The God of Jacob

by Theodore H. Epp

Director
Back to the Bible Broadcast

A
BACK TO THE BIBLE
PUBLICATION

Back to the Bible
Lincoln, Nebraska 68501

65,000 printed to date—1983
(5-1921—65M—83)
ISBN 0-8474-1230-X

Printed in the United States of America

Foreword

In the title *The God of Jacob,* the emphasis is on the word "God." The man involved was important only as he permitted God to reveal Himself through his life. In Jacob's life we see the long-suffering and patience of God in molding a man into what He wants him to be. When God begins to work in a person's life, He does not stop until He is finished. This is clearly seen in the life of Jacob.

The biographical study of this man is not left on the parched pages of history. It is brought home pointedly to the 20th-century Christian. Jacob was not perfect. He was mightily used of God, but he also had great weaknesses. The present-day believer will be encouraged to realize that if God could use this man, He can work mightily in his life also.

One distinctive quality of Jacob's life was his restless faith. Somewhere in the life of this man, every believer will undoubtedly find himself. From the pages of this book you will gain a new appreciation of how God is able to take what the world considers foolish and use it to put to shame what the world considers wise. You will thrill at the ways of God as you see how He worked out His sovereign plan through a human vessel. The study of the life of Jacob will give you a clearer concept of who God is and what He wants to do through your life.

As Theodore Epp prepared these messages—first for radio, then in book form—his main burden was that believers might realize that the God of Jacob is their God also. Mr. Epp, through the urging of the Spirit in his own life, was especially concerned that all of us might realize that this same God—unchanged—is just as powerful and great in meeting our needs as He was in meeting the needs of Jacob. It is wonderful to be able to say, "This same God is our God." It is even more wonderful to be able to say, "This same God is *my* God."

May this book cause you to exclaim in worship, "How fathomless the depths of God's resources, wisdom, and knowledge! How unsearchable His decisions, and how mysterious His methods! For who has ever understood the thoughts of the Lord, or has ever been His adviser? Or who has ever advanced God anything to have Him pay him back? For from Him everything comes, through Him everything lives, and for Him everything exists. Glory to Him forever! Amen" (Rom. 11:33-36, Williams).

—*The Publishers*

Contents

Chapter	Page
1. The God of Abraham, Isaac and Jacob	7
2. The God of Jacob	18
3. Jacob's Birth	23
4. The Birthright	27
5. The Stolen Blessing	36
6. Blessing and Reaping	50
7. Twenty Years of Discipline	59
8. Jacob's Departure From Haran	68
9. The Carnal Man Becomes a Spiritual Man	76
10. After Peniel	97
11. Bethel at Last	112
12. The School of Sorrow	124
13. Victorious Faith in the Retiring Years	130

Chapter 1

The God of Abraham, Isaac and Jacob

It is not enough just to know information about the Bible. We must relate the Word of God to our lives. Even more than that, we must relate the eternal God to our lives.

The Scriptures speak of the God of Abraham, the God of Isaac and the God of Jacob. Is He really your God too? Perhaps you wonder how you can relate the God of Abraham, Isaac and Jacob to your life. It will become obvious to you, however, as you see what the Scriptures have to say about God and His relationship with these three men.

God told Moses, "I am the God of thy father, the God of Abraham, the God of Isaac, and the God of Jacob" (Ex. 3:6). When Moses heard this, he "hid his face; for he was afraid to look upon God." Exodus 3:6 is not the only place in Scripture where God is referred to as the God of Abraham, Isaac and Jacob. In the New Testament, Christ Himself referred to this description of God when He asked the Sadducees, "But as touching the resurrection of the dead, have ye not read that which was spoken unto you by God, saying, I am the God of Abraham, and the God of Isaac, and the God of Jacob? God is not the God of the dead, but of the living" (Matt. 22:31,32). Notice especially Christ's statement that "God is not the God of the dead, but of the living." This same Almighty God is living today. Through faith in Him, every person can be delivered from condemnation and can have God residing in his life to produce fruit by His Spirit (John 5:24; 15:5).

Not only is God still living, but His Word is living also. Hebrews 4:12 says, "For the Word that God speaks is alive and active: it cuts more keenly than any two-edged sword: it strikes through to the place where soul and spirit meet, to the innermost intimacies of a man's being: it exposes the very

7

thoughts and motives of a man's heart" (Phillips). If there
were no other proof of the inspiration of the Scriptures, this
is sufficient—the Word of God lives. The longer I study the
Bible and dig deeper into it, the more it does for my heart.
One of the multitude of blessings I have received from the
Word of God is the realization that the God of Abraham,
Isaac and Jacob is the same God I serve. You, too, will be
greatly encouraged as we study the living Word and see that
this same God can be your God too.

As we consider man's creation and his fall into sin, we are
taken back to Genesis—the book of origins, or beginnings.
Everything but God Himself can be traced back to the Book
of Genesis. This book gives us the beginning of the universe,
life, man, covenants, marriage, sin, redemption, death,
nations, governments, music, art, literature, agriculture,
mechanics, cities, languages, and so on.

Man was created to be a companion to God. This is a
significant truth to remember throughout our study. We
must never forget God's original intention for man—that of
relationship and fellowship with Himself. Genesis 1:26,27
tells us, "And God said, Let us make man in our image, after
our likeness: and let them have dominion over the fish of the
sea, and over the fowl of the air, and over the cattle, and over
all the earth, and over every creeping thing that creepeth
upon the earth. So God created man in his own image, in the
image of God created he him; male and female created he
them." Thus we see that man is the offspring of God. As
such, he is related to God in different ways.

Related by Creation

Man is directly related to God by creation because he was
created by God. Because God made man, He alone perfectly
understands man. So also God is the only One who can
perfectly govern man because He knows every detail about
every person.

When we look upon ourselves as fallen people, we find it
hard to understand how there has ever been a close relationship between people and God. Sin broke this relationship,
and even after the relationship is restored, it is strained by
sin. As we consider God's purpose in creating man and then
see how man has been alienated from God, we are compelled

to wonder how a true fellowship with God could ever exist again. It is only logical for each of us to ask, How can I really have fellowship with such a holy God, who was the God of Abraham, the God of Isaac and the God of Jacob? But we *can* have fellowship with God even as these great patriarchs of the faith had.

Related by Authority

We can have an intimate fellowship with God because He, in His sovereign power, governs us. In fact, man cannot live apart from God. Colossians 1:16,17 tells us, "For it was through him that everything was made, whether spiritual or material, seen or unseen. Through him, and for him, also, were created power and dominion, ownership and authority. In fact, every single thing was created through, and for, him. He is both the first principle and the upholding principle of the whole scheme of creation" (Phillips). God is not only the Creator but also the upholding principle of the whole creation. As we consider man's degeneracy in contrast to the holiness of God, we are forced to ask, Is there any hope? Can man—can I—actually have an intimate relationship with God?

As we trace man's history after his fall into sin, it looks more and more doubtful that a harmonious relationship between God and man could ever exist again. The third chapter of Genesis records man's fall into sin, the fourth chapter tells of the first recorded murder, chapters 6-8 describe the terrible destruction of the universal flood, and chapter 11 relates man's attempt to build the Tower of Babel in defiance of God. But God is not dead. And because He is living and because He is God, He had a plan for restoring man's fellowship with Himself.

Concerning Christ, we are told in Colossians that "he is the head of the body which is the Church. Life from nothing began through him, and life from the dead began through him, and he is, therefore, justly called the Lord of all. It was in him that the full nature of God chose to live, and through him God planned to reconcile in his own person, as it were, everything on earth and everything in Heaven by virtue of the sacrifice of the cross. ... This reconciliation assumes, of course, that you maintain a firm position in the faith, and do not allow yourselves to be shifted away from the hope of the gospel, which you have heard, and which, indeed, the whole world is now having an opportunity of hearing. I myself have been made a minister of the same gospel" (1:18-20,23, Phillips).

Christ originated physical life through His creative powers. Man now has physical life, but because of his fall into sin he is spiritually dead. But just as Christ was able to produce life from nothing, so also He is able to bring life out of death. Therefore, He is "justly called the Lord of all" (v. 18). Through Christ every person is made reconcilable to God. Because of what He did on the cross, every person can be reconciled to God by receiving Jesus Christ as his personal Saviour.

There is no room for any wavering of faith here. There was a wavering of faith in Genesis 3 when the Devil, through the serpent, said to Eve, "Yea, hath God said, Ye shall not eat of every tree of the garden?" (v. 1). Later, in verse 4, the Devil told her, "Ye shall not surely die." This was the opposite of what the Lord had told Adam and Eve: "But of the tree of the knowledge of good and evil, thou shalt not eat of it: for in the day that thou eatest thereof thou shalt surely die" (2:17). Satan is the great slanderer and liar. Jesus Himself said of him, "He is a liar, and the father of it" (John 8:44). Truly one begins to wonder if there is any hope for man. Because of a lack of faith, Adam and Eve disobeyed God. But at the cross, faith and obedience are joined together, resulting in a wonderful restoration of man's relationship to God. Our greatest need is to trust and obey.

The requirement to trust and obey is so simple and yet so profound. It is the very heart of true Christianity. In fact, we can call it the "law of faith." In using the word "law" I am not referring to the Old Testament Law but to a principle that is always true, such as the law of gravity. The law of faith is the basis on which God can work out His will in man, and man can demonstrate through his life the salvation he has received from God.

That faith is the basis on which God works is also seen from a study of the lives of Abraham, Isaac and Jacob. The fundamental truth is that man can realize his own God-created life only by trusting God and walking in His way by true obedience. Thus, from the life stories of these men, we see through God's revelation that He is seeking to restore people to obedience by restoring them to the main principle of human life—that of faith in Himself. God is the God of the living, and it is only through faith in Him that individuals can be restored to a true relationship with God.

Kinds of Faith

God was willing to call Himself the God of Abraham, Isaac and Jacob. He was willing to be called the God of these three men even though they were very different in character and had a great variance in their faith response to God. Abraham's faith was an obedient faith, whereas Isaac's faith was a passive faith. Jacob, on the other hand, had a restless faith.

Somewhere in these three principal characters of the Old Testament, I am sure you will find demonstrated the kind of faith you have. You will see yourself described in Abraham if you have a great and obedient faith. You will find God doing great things for you in spite of the fact that He will take you through many trials. Or perhaps you see yourself with a faith like Isaac's. He had a passive faith and did not do great, outstanding things as the world measures them. If yours is a restless faith and if you are unable to wait for God to work, you will find yourself described in Jacob.

In Hebrews 4:9-11 we are told, "There still exists, therefore, a full and complete rest for the people of God. And he who experiences his rest is resting from his own work as fully as God from his. Let us then be eager to know this rest for ourselves, and let us beware that no one misses it through falling into the same kind of unbelief as those we have mentioned" (Phillips). In other words, when we believe God as He is revealed through His Word, we will find the full and complete rest that He has for His people.

Faith has different forms of expression. Abraham's faith always took the form of unquestioned obedience. Abraham made many mistakes, but he had an obedient faith that did not question God. Isaac was different. His faith took the form of passive expression. God spoke to him merely to ratify what He had already said to Abraham. Nothing especially new was given to Isaac. Rather than an acting faith, his faith was more the kind that accepted without resisting. He was submissive to his father and to God, but he performed no great acts of adventuring faith himself. Yet God chooses to be called "the God of Isaac" as well as "the God of Abraham."

Jacob was altogether different from Abraham and Isaac. His faith was expressed in restlessness—he could not wait on God. The communications from God always came to Jacob after a period of spiritual wandering, and their purpose was to restore his fellowship with God.

Even though the faith of these three men took different forms of expression, we must recognize that at least they all did exercise faith. Abraham's was an obedient faith, Isaac's was a passive faith, and Jacob's was a restless faith. Yet there was faith. God was able to work in remaking these men because they were men of faith. They were able to find their way back into conscious relationship with God because of their faith. So again we see that faith is the basis on which God works out His will in man. Also, it is through faith that man is enabled to realize the will of God.

In Romans 12:1,2 we see the relationship between an obedient faith and discovering the will of God. Paul wrote: "I beseech you therefore, brethren, by the mercies of God, that ye present your bodies a living sacrifice, holy, acceptable unto God, which is your reasonable service. And be not conformed to this world: but be ye transformed by the renewing of your mind, that ye may prove what is that good, and acceptable, and perfect, will of God."

When we have an obedient faith, we will present our bodies and renew our minds as we are instructed. The result will be our discovering or proving what is God's good, acceptable and perfect will. God will reveal His will to us when we are obedient to Him. As we are obedient in one step, God will show us the next step. From the lives of Abraham, Isaac and Jacob we see the importance of living by faith one step at a time. Man can find himself and realize the true meaning of his own life only as he places his confidence in God and obeys Him with unquestioning loyalty.

You, too, can establish a conscious relationship with God by obedient faith. You will not be able to salvage the years you have wasted, but you can go forward with God from this point if you will serve Him through an obedient faith. If you have sinned and have not yet confessed that sin to God, you should do so now so you can move forward with Him. The Word of God promises that "if we confess our sins, he is faithful and just to forgive us our sins, and to cleanse us from all unrighteousness" (I John 1:9).

Remember that the God who identifies Himself as the God of Abraham, Isaac and Jacob also identifies Himself as your God and my God. However, in order to have this vital relationship and fellowship with Him, we must have an obedient faith that takes God at His word and acts accordingly.

Notice the promises in II Corinthians 6:17,18: "Wherefore come out from among them, and be ye separate, saith the Lord, and touch not the unclean thing; and I will receive you, and will be a Father unto you, and ye shall be my sons and daughters, saith the Lord Almighty." When we are obedient to God in doing what He says, He promises three things: "I will receive you, and will be a Father unto you, and ye shall be my sons and daughters." The same truth is emphasized in Revelation 21:7: "He that overcometh shall inherit all things; and I will be his God, and he shall be my son." All of this results from an obedient faith.

The lives of Abraham, Isaac and Jacob show the significance of the phrase, "The just shall live by faith" (Rom. 1:17). This statement was first recorded in Habakkuk 2:4 and is also mentioned in Galatians 3:11 and Hebrews 10:38. It is an irrefutable scriptural principle that those who are justified are to live on the basis of faith. That this principle underlies our entire relationship with God is seen from Hebrews 11:6: "But without faith it is impossible to please him: for he that cometh to God must believe that he is, and that he is a rewarder of them that diligently seek him." This means there is hope for you. You can have God's blessing on your life and experience intimate fellowship with Him if you will exercise your faith in Him and take Him at His word.

The Response to God's Communications

God's communications to Abraham, Isaac and Jacob were distintively different. He commuicated differently with each man. Why? Because He knew them. And He knows all the details about your life and mine, and He knows how to deal with us.

There were seven divine communications with Abraham, each initiating a significant move forward. Abraham responded with an obedient faith—he obeyed God.

There were only two divine communications to Isaac. The purpose of these was to ratify what had already been told to Abraham. No special call was given to Isaac nor was any specific action asked of him. Isaac was not discontent, however, for he accepted these things obediently and waited upon God.

There were five divine communications with Jacob, and in each of them God arrested Jacob's activity and changed the order of his life. Jacob was usually doing something he shouldn't—either running ahead of God or backsliding—and God came to him, halted him in his ways and redirected his life. Jacob had a restless faith. Nevertheless, he became obedient.

God Communicates With Abraham

As we consider each of these men in more detail, we notice that the first communication to Abraham was a call to leave his country and to set his face toward a new land with new conditions of life. God told Abraham (whose name was Abram at that time), "Get thee out of thy country, and from thy kindred, and from thy father's house, unto a land that I will shew thee" (Gen. 12:1). This is all the information Abraham had about the land he was to seek. Abraham moved slowly at first, but after a time he came to the land of Canaan.

After Abraham had come to the land, God communicated a second time with him and said, "I will make of thee a great nation, and I will bless thee, and make thy name great; and thou shalt be a blessing: and I will bless them that bless thee, and curse him that curseth thee: and in thee shall all families of the earth be blessed" (vv. 2,3). In addition to promising Abraham a land, God promised him descendants and a blessing. But at this time it was only a promise. All Abraham could do was wait on God in faith.

God's third communication with Abraham resulted in the land's being given to him directly, but under very interesting and remarkable circumstances of faith. There was a quarrel between his herdsmen and the herdsmen of Lot. Knowing it would be better for them to live in different places, Abraham gave Lot his choice of the land. After Lot and his herdsmen had departed from Abraham, God said to Abraham, "Lift up now thine eyes, and look from the place where thou art northward, and southward, and eastward, and westward: for all the land which thou seest, to thee will I give it, and to thy seed for ever. And I will make thy seed as the dust of the earth: so that if a man can number the dust of the earth, then shall thy seed also be numbered. Arise, walk through the land in the length of it and in the breadth of it; for I will give it unto thee" (13:14-17).

In His fourth communication with Abraham, God promised him a seed that would become a great nation. Up until then He had simply said, "Unto thy seed." No further details had been given. Abraham asked God, "Lord God, what wilt thou give me, seeing I go childless, and the steward of my house is this Eliezer of Damascus? And Abram said, Behold, to me thou hast given no seed: and, lo, one born in my house is mine heir" (15:2,3). God graciously answered Abraham, "This shall not be thine heir; but he that shall come forth out of thine own bowels shall be thine heir" (v. 4). God had now become more specific to Abraham regarding his descendants.

In the fifth communication with Abraham, God reiterated His solemn covenant with Abraham and gave circumcision as the sign of the covenant. God's covenant with Abraham was an unconditional one and could not be broken.

God's sixth communicaton with Abraham was a final and direct promise of the birth of a son in the following year. God told Abraham, "I will certainly return unto thee according to the time of life, and, lo, Sarah thy wife shall have a son" (18:10).

The seventh and final communication of God with Abraham was when God tested Abraham's faith regarding the offering of his son Isaac. Genesis 22 deals with this crucial time in Abraham's life.

In these seven communications God led Abraham through circumstances that became more and more trying. Because Abraham followed by faith, God was able to lead him on to

higher experiences and larger possessions that were not just
associated with the earth. Anything that Abraham sacri-
ficed so that he might enjoy the fellowship of God was
reduced to nothing in view of what he received. He was
loaded daily with God's benefits. He forsook a home, but he
received a country. He cut himself off from the past, but he
entered into the present with all God's provisions and into
the future with all God's promises. He forfeited an inheritance of his forefathers, but he received eternal treasures. He
lived in a tent in the wilderness instead of a roofed house in
Ur, but he gained for himself a city whose builder and maker
was God. It is always so.

The only reason God deprives man is that He might make
room for something better. All of this is given to us in God's
Word that we may benefit from the experiences of others.
First Corinthians 10:11 reminds us that "these things happened unto them for ensamples: and they are written for our
admonition, upon whom the ends of the world are come."

God Communicates With Isaac

In contrast to Abraham, Isaac led a very simple life—
unassuming and uneventful. In the quietness of his life,
Isaac had two communications from God. In the first, God
revealed to him that the covenant made with Abraham
should continue in him. No action was called for on Isaac's
part. The only requirement necessary was a faith in God to
do what He had promised. Genesis 26:1-5 tells us about this
communication with Isaac. God commanded him not to go
down into Egypt but to dwell in the land of Canaan. God
promised Isaac, "I will make thy seed to multiply as the stars
of heaven, and will give unto thy seed all these countries;
and in thy seed shall all the nations of the earth be blessed"
(v. 4).

God communicated with Isaac the second time for the
purpose of ratifying the same covenant. The Lord appeared
to Isaac and said, "I am the God of Abraham thy father: fear
not, for I am with thee, and will bless thee, and multiply thy
seed for my servant Abraham's sake" (v. 24).

Thus we see that Isaac was a quiet type of person—restful
and passive. His life was not characterized by actions of
magnificence nor by great daring triumphs. God never broke

in on Isaac's life with the thick darkness of trial that Abraham passed through or with the alarming struggle at Peniel that Jacob experienced. Although Isaac had a quiet and simple life, he, too, was included in the covenant and received covenant privileges. Isaac, the well digger, was necessary in God's great plan and economy.

It is important to remember that we are all needed in God's great plan. It is not necessary for everyone to be a trailblazer or a pioneer of faith as Abraham was. God calls some for this type of work, and I am thankful He called us to venture out as pioneers of faith regarding the Back to the Bible Broadcast. But God has not called everyone to do this type of work.

God Communicates With Jacob

Neither should everyone be like Jacob, a man with a restless spirit who was never securely anchored in God until he was crippled at Peniel. God dealt with Jacob in an entirely different manner because Jacob was an entirely different type of person. The greatest aspect of Jacob's life was that he believed God. Nevertheless, he was a man of restless activity because he had a restless faith. The five communications of God with him were all for the purpose of checking him, correcting his methods and keeping him in the pathway of the divine will. Whereas God dealt with Abraham so that he might move forward in new adventures of faith, God had to deal with Jacob in order to correct him.

From this brief, overall view of Abraham, Isaac and Jacob, we now focus attention on the details of Jacob's life. We especially want to see why God was pleased to refer to Himself as "the God of Jacob" (Ex. 3:6).

Chapter 2

The God of Jacob

Jacob and Esau were the sons of Isaac and Rebekah. In these two sons was the beginning of two different nations that have been in continuous conflict throughout the centuries. These two sons also represent the conflict of the flesh and the Spirit.

Esau represents that which is natural, whereas Jacob represents that which is spritual. The conflict between the natural and the spiritual is present in every believer's heart. It is the conflict of the two natures. The Scriptures say, "The flesh lusteth against the Spirit, and the Spirit against the flesh: and these are contrary the one to the other: so that ye cannot do the things that ye would" (Gal. 5:17). However, believers are encouraged to realize that, because of the greatness of God, the Spirit will ultimately triumph and the flesh will be brought into subjection.

In Esau we see the profane nature that despises the riches and promises of God. In Jacob we see the desire for that which is godly, even though he used fleshly (carnal) methods to attain the benefit of the promises.

In comparing Abraham, Isaac and Jacob, the Scriptures present Abraham as a trailblazer—a pioneer of faith. He had an active faith and experienced many great triumphs of faith. Isaac was a totally different type of person. He had a passive faith. Although he had his weaknesses, he was a firm believer in God. When God revealed his weaknesses to him, Isaac became stalwart in faith. He was an unassuming type of man—meek, humble, submissive. Abraham was a leader; Isaac was a follower.

Jacob's life was one of conflict. In him we see the conflict between the flesh and the Spirit. This is the key to understanding his life. Jacob's life strikingly exhibits the power of the old nature, but it also exhibits the power of God's love and grace. In Jacob we see the utter worthlessness and depravity of the human nature, but we also see the deepest instruction as to God's purpose and infinite grace.

Have you sometimes wondered why God has been so careful to tell us the weaknesses of a person's character as well as his strengths? God has recorded both the good and the bad things about Jacob. He has done this to magnify the riches of divine grace and to admonish us not to follow in the carnal footsteps of this patriarch. God has not recorded Jacob's sins in order to perpetuate their memory, for He has blotted out Jacob's sins forever—even as He does those of the believer today who confesses his sins. God tells us both the good and the bad things about Jacob so we can see him as he really was.

By contrast, the majority of human biographers gloss over the errors and infirmities of those about whom they write. Their biographies often tend to discourage the reader rather than edify him, for the main characters are not believable— they do not seem to be real persons. I have read such biographies and have been greatly challenged to live like the persons I have read about, only to discover I couldn't do it. Historians mostly emphasize the achievements, not the discouragements, heartaches and trials, of their characters. Thus, they are histories of what people ought to have been, not of what they really were. Biographers are not able to look into the souls of the people they write about and see the carnalities there. However, in the Bible God shows us both the strengths and the weaknesses of a person's character so that we can see the same struggles in his life as we have in ours.

Believers grow weary of the conflict between the flesh and the Spirit, and some wonder when the inner struggle will end. As long as we are in these earthly bodies, our two natures will struggle. As we walk with God we will learn what to expect of the old nature and how to cope with it, but the conflict will always be there. Thus, God gives us the whole picture of Jacob's life so that we might see this conflict and learn for ourselves. As God worked with Jacob, little by little He was able to instill in his heart the realization that

are is totally depraved and that nothing good can
d of it. This is true not only of Jacob but also of all
braham lied to Abimelech when he was in Gerar
(see   . 20:1,2), and Isaac lied about the same thing when
he was in Gerar (see 26:6,7). Isaac succumbed to the scheming of Rebekah and Jacob. Nothing good can be expected of
the old nature.

Jacob's True Nature

In the biblical record, God reveals Jacob's true nature—
both his deep-seated, inner longing for God's best and his
human scheming and carnal methods of attaining it. God's
infinite grace is revealed to us as we see how He continued
lavishing on Jacob His unwearied and uncompromising
love. Nothing in Jacob merited all of this—even as nothing
in us merits God's love and grace. Although Jacob continued
to sin, God continued to work with him in patient love. God
continued to pour out His love on Jacob, while never once
condoning his sins. For many years God allowed Jacob to
pursue the path he had chosen. Thus, Jacob learned better
lessons because of his spirit of independence. He saw the cost
of trying to live his life apart from God. Jacob wanted the
things of God, but he wanted them in his own way and in his
own time. Jacob found it almost impossible to wait for God to
work out His will in His own time.

Jacob's selfishness, which manifested itself many times,
became his own rod of chastening. In patient love, God
always followed Jacob, until finally Jacob came to the end of
himself.

God loved Jacob, but He hated his sin and carnality. The
life of Jacob is not a demonstration of man's perseverance
with God as much as it is a demonstration of God's perseverance with man. God's perseverance with His own people is
also evident in the way He worked with the Israelites. He
was with His people for 40 years in the desert. After they had
come into the land of Canaan they became engrossed in idol
worship, and God had to send them into Babylonian cap-
tivity to teach them severe lessons. God was with them all
the while, and by the time He was through with them they
had learned their lessons well. After the Babylonian cap-
tivity, widespread idol worship was never again known

among the Hebrew nation. God always finishes what He begins. The Word of God assures us, "Being confident of this very thing, that he which hath begun a good work in you will perform it until the day of Jesus Christ" (Phil. 1:6). God's principle of finishing what He begins is clearly seen in the life of Jacob.

If we had been choosing a man to lead a nation, I am sure we would not have chosen Jacob. He was a schemer and crooked in so many ways as he sought to gain both material and spiritual blessings. However, we have to realize that Jacob's environment was not the best. Isaac loved Esau more, whereas Rebekah loved Jacob more. With such division in the family, it is understandable that the result would be serious conflict. Rebekah helped Jacob deceive his father—she felt the end justified the means. On the other hand, Esau belittled and despised that which was spiritual. What blessing can be expected from such a family of conflict?

But God

In cases like Jacob's God delights to work. He starts where there is no promise of anything and produces something for His glory. In His sovereign will, God laid His hand on Jacob for a special purpose. When God undertakes something, no one can defeat Him. It took 30 years for God to accomplish His purpose with Jacob, but when He finished, He had the kind of man He desired.

God transformed Jacob into a prince. This is all the more significant when you realize the Bible refers to Jacob as a worm. Isaiah 41:14 says, "Fear not, thou worm Jacob, and ye men of Israel; I will help thee, saith the Lord, and thy redeemer, the Holy One of Israel." What is weaker and more worthless than a worm? This is what God thought of Jacob. But God stooped to associate Himself with one of the weakest and least attractive of our human race. God chose to transform Jacob from a worm into a prince. This gives us the key regarding God's choice of Jacob. The warped character of Jacob provided a suitable background for the display of God's grace.

If God chose only the strong, the noble and the brilliant, the vast majority of us would be disqualified. But it pleases

God to choose what the world considers foolish in order to confound the wisdom of the world. The Apostle Paul wrote: "Because the foolishness of God is wiser than men; and the weakness of God is stronger than men. For ye see your calling, brethren, how that not many wise men after the flesh, not many mighty, not many noble, are called: but God hath chosen the foolish things of the world to confound the wise; and God hath chosen the weak things of the world to confound the things which are mighty; and base things of the world, and things which are despised, hath God chosen, yea, and things which are not, to bring to nought things that are: that no flesh should glory in his presence" (I Cor. 1:25-29).

Psalm 22 prophesied of Christ, "I am a worm, and no man; a reproach of men, and despised of the people. All they that see me laugh me to scorn: they shoot out the lip, they shake the head, saying, He trusted on the Lord that he would deliver him: let him deliver him, seeing he delighted in him" (vv. 6-8). It was even prophesied of Jesus Christ Himself that He would be a worm in the eyes of the world; yet He provided salvation for the sins of the world. The wisdom of the world was confounded by God.

None of us is worthy of God's grace and mercy, but it pleases Him to choose us so He might display His glory through us. This is why He chose Jacob—to make a prince out of a worm.

How wonderful it is that God condescends to be called "the God of Jacob." Only God could see the princely qualities in this man. He delights to begin where others have given up in despair. Perhaps you do not see anything of value in your life. Give God a chance to make you into what He wants you to be. Perhaps you value your life too highly; thus, you do not realize your need of God. But if you see nothing in your life, then there is hope. God delights to work in such a life. Yield yourself to God so He might do His perfect work in you.

Chapter 3

Jacob's Birth

Jacob was a miracle child. Abraham and Sarah had waited 25 years for Isaac to be born, and Isaac and Rebekah waited 20 years for the birth of Jacob. Genesis 25:21,22 says, "Isaac intreated the Lord for his wife, because she was barren: and the Lord was intreated of him, and Rebekah his wife conceived. And the children struggled together within her; and she said, If it be so, why am I thus? And she went to enquire of the Lord." Rebekah did not know she was going to give birth to twins, and she could not understand what the trouble was. God allowed this to happen to her so He could reveal His plan for the children she would bear.

God explained to Rebekah, "Two nations are in thy womb, and two manner of people shall be separated from thy bowels; and the one people shall be stronger than the other people; and the elder shall serve the younger" (v. 23). God told Rebekah that two nations would come into existence through her two children. Those nations would be in conflict, just as the two babies were in conflict in her womb.

Romans 9:13 makes a startling statement: "Jacob have I loved, but Esau have I hated." The words "loved" and "hated" are not words of emotion so much as they are words of extreme comparison. They are also used in the comparative sense in Luke 14:26: "If any man come to me, and hate not his father, and mother, and wife, and children, and brethren, and sisters, yea, and his own life also, he cannot be my disciple." The word "hate" in this verse is used in a different way than it is commonly used today. The Lord was emphasizing that our love for relatives and self should seem like hate in comparison to our love for Him.

In Romans 9:13 the matter of choice seems to be emphasized also through the strong words of contrast. In God's
sovereign grace and eternal purpose, He chose Jacob and the
nation that would come into existence through him. The
context of Romans 9 tells us, "And not only this; but when
Rebecca [Rebekah] also had conceived by one, even by our
father Isaac; (for the children being not yet born, neither
having done any good or evil, that the purpose of God
according to election might stand, not of works, but of him
that calleth;) it was said unto her, The elder shall serve the
younger. As it is written, Jacob have I loved, but Esau have I
hated" (vv. 10-13).

This does not mean that Esau was condemned before his
birth, but it does emphasize the extreme contrast in God's
relationship with these two men. Because God had chosen
Jacob, His dealings with Esau seemed to be hatred in
comparison.

The choice between the two individuals involved two nations because two nations were to descend from Jacob and
Esau. God chose the Israelites, not the Edomites, to fulfill His
plan. God's choice was not made on the basis of merit but according to His sovereign grace before the twins were born.

Faith, not merit, is the principle of sonship. God knew that
Esau would not have faith; therefore, he was not chosen. God
is not arbitrary or biased in His choosing—nor can we
charge Him with favoritism. God's choice between Jacob
and Esau was not based on favoritism but on discernment.

Another of God's choices is referred to in I Peter 1:2: "Elect
according to the foreknowledge of God the Father." The
word "elect" means "to choose." Election is according to the
foreknowledge of God and is wholly of grace, apart from all
human merit. Election proceeds from divine volition, for we
are told in John 15:16, "Ye have not chosen me, but I have
chosen you." Verse 19 of the same chapter records Christ's
words: "I have chosen you out of the world."

I believe election is the sovereign act of God whereby certain persons are chosen for distinctive services for Him. It
primarily involves service, not salvation. Esau could have
placed his faith in God and perhaps did, but the Scriptures
do not indicate that he did. God knew Jacob and Esau before
their birth.

Jacob's Spiritual Conflict

In spite of Jacob's meanness and trickery, he had a genuine concern for spiritual things. He often violated his spiritual desires, but he persisted in wanting to grow spiritually, and God continued to deal with him. One key factor in Jacob's life is that, in spite of his many weaknesses and failures, he had great aspirations concerning the things of God.

By contrast, Esau was outwardly attractive and generous; yet inwardly he despised heavenly values. He preferred to gratify his sensual desires rather than pursue or develop spiritual values.

God knew all of this about Jacob and Esau before they were born. Thus, He was fully able to make a choice between them before their birth.

Even the birth of Jacob and Esau shows their great difference in character. Genesis 25:24-26 says, "When her days to be delivered were fulfilled, behold, there were twins in her womb. And the first came out red, all over like an hairy garment; and they called his name Esau. And after that came his brother out, and his hand took hold on Esau's heel; and his name was called Jacob: and Isaac was threescore years old when she bare them" (Gen. 25:24-26).

Because the firstborn was hairy, he was called "Esau," which means "hairy." The second son was named "Jacob," which means "supplanter." When Jacob came out of the womb, he took hold of Esau's heel. This was symbolic of his life, for Jacob went through life taking advantage of others—tripping them up so he could get ahead.

In character, Esau was a shallow person. Hebrews 12:16 refers to him as a "profane person." The word "profane" means "impious" or "unhallowed." In Esau we see the old nature symbolized; at times it looks good outwardly, but it is inwardly corrupt. There is no record that Esau ever worshiped or was concerned about his relationship with God.

In Jacob we see both natures and the conflict that waged between them. Jacob not only demonstrated the old nature that he inherited from Adam, but he also demonstrated the new nature because of his faith in God. Hosea 12:3,4 emphasizes the conflict in Jacob's life: "He took his brother by the heel in the womb, and by his strength he had power with God: yea, he had power over the angel, and prevailed: he wept, and made supplication unto him: he found him in Beth-el, and there he spake with us."

People customarily look at that which is worst in others, but God always searches out the best so that He might perfect it in the person's life. God saw in Jacob tremendous spiritual possibilities and worked with him for 30 years to develop his potential.

The differences between Jacob and Esau became more prominent as they grew older. Genesis 25:27 says, "And the boys grew: and Esau was a cunning hunter, a man of the field; and Jacob was a plain man, dwelling in tents." Esau loved the outdoors—he was "a man of the field." By contrast, Jacob was "a plain man, dwelling in tents."

The word "plain" is from a Hebrew word that is translated "perfect" nine times in the *King James Version*. It does not refer to sinless perfection but to one who is right with God. However, the word "plain" as used to describe Jacob seems also to emphasize a disposition that found pleasure in the quiet life of home—in contrast to the wild hunter's life led by Esau. The context of Genesis 25:27 emphasizes Jacob's personal desires rather than his spiritual character.

The significance of tent dwelling has been pointed out in regard to Abraham's life. Hebrews 11:9,10 says of Abraham, "By faith he sojourned in the land of promise, as in a strange country, dwelling in tabernacles [tents] with Isaac and Jacob, the heirs with him of the same promise: for he looked for a city which hath foundations, whose builder and maker is God." A person who realized he was a stranger and pilgrim in a country lived in a tent. Spiritually, this was true of Abraham and Jacob but not of Esau. This points out to us again the spiritual desires Jacob had, even though he fell so far short so many times. His spiritual aspirations provided God with the basis for His continual working in Jacob's life and for the disciplines that were to shape his character. Despite Jacob's failures, there was always the undercurrent of faith. This also helps explain what is meant by God's statement: "Jacob have I loved, but Esau have I hated" (Rom. 9:13).

Chapter 4

The Birthright

The first pact made between Esau and Jacob as grown men concerned the birthright. The boys had grown up in a home of conflict because their parents were guilty of favoritism. The Scriptures point out that "Isaac loved Esau, because he did eat of his venison: but Rebekah loved Jacob" (Gen. 25:28). Before the birth of the children, God had told Rebekah that "the elder shall serve the younger" (v. 23). No doubt this was common knowledge in the family and resulted in even more conflict.

In Old Testament times the birthright was a most cherished possession. It involved dignity, power and usually a double portion of the inheritance, plus other special blessings. Concerning the birthright, C. I. Scofield wrote: "The 'birthright' had three elements: (1) Until the establishment of the Aaronic priesthood, the head of the family exercised priestly rights. (2) The Abrahamic family held the Edenic promise of the Satan-Bruiser (Gen. 3.15)—Abel, Seth, Shem, Abraham, Isaac, *Esau.* (3) Esau, as the firstborn, was in the direct line of the Abrahamic promise of the Earth-Blesser (Gen. 12.3). For all that was revealed, in Esau might have been fulfilled those two great Messianic promises" (*The Scofield Reference Bible,* p. 38).

Esau's sale of the birthright is recorded in Genesis 25:29-34: "And Jacob sod [boiled] pottage: and Esau came from the field, and he was faint: and Esau said to Jacob, Feed me, I pray thee, with that same red pottage; for I am faint: therefore was his name called Edom. And Jacob said, Sell me this day thy birthright. And Esau said, Behold, I am at the point to die: and what profit shall this birthright do to me? And Jacob said, Swear to me this day; and he sware

unto him: and he sold his birthright unto Jacob. Then Jacob
gave Esau bread and pottage of lentiles; and he did eat and
drink, and rose up, and went his way: thus Esau despised his
birthright."

Jacob had been waiting for an opportunity to get the
birthright from Esau. Jacob could have rightfully expected
the birthright since God had promised that the elder would
serve the younger, but Jacob's methods of obtaining it were
entirely wrong. Jacob sought the right thing in the wrong
way. Using carnal methods to attain spiritual goals is never
acceptable to God. Jacob felt that the end justified the
means.

In this incident we see the value of waiting for God. The
birthright was Jacob's by God's determinate will, and, in
due time, He would have given it to Jacob. Although Jacob
connived to get the birthright, it was 30 years later before he
actually benefited from it. Jacob knew the importance of
believing God, but he did not know the importance of waiting on God.

We also need to learn the discipline of patiently waiting on
God to fulfill His will in His own time. God's Word says,
"Cast not away therefore your confidence, which hath great
recompence of reward. For ye have need of patience, that,
after ye have done the will of God, ye might receive the
promise" (Heb. 10:35,36).

Although Jacob schemed to get possession of the birthright, God did not permit him to receive its benefits until he
first acknowledged Esau as the rightful, original owner.
How different Jacob's life would have been if he had
patiently waited on God to give him the birthright.

Jacob watched for his opportunity to catch his brother off
guard so he could get the birthright from him. The time came
when Esau returned from the field completely exhausted.
Esau thought he was about to starve, and he was willing to
do almost anything to get something to eat. Jacob took
advantage of the opportunity. He offered Esau something to
eat if Esau would sell him his birthright.

The Bargain of the Brothers

As Esau thought about Jacob's proposition, he said,
"Behold, I am at the point to die: and what profit shall this

birthright do to me?" (Gen. 25:32). With an attitude like this, Esau was an easy victim for Jacob, who said, "Swear to me this day; and he sware unto him: and he sold his birthright unto Jacob" (v. 33).

The Scriptures conclude the account of the sale of the birthright by saying, "Then Jacob gave Esau bread and pottage of lentiles; and he did eat and drink, and rose up, and went his way: thus Esau despised his birthright" (v. 34). The meal was served and eaten—and God's evaluation of Esau's action was recorded.

In selling his birthright, Esau revealed his true character. Notice especially his words recorded in verse 32: "I am at the point to die: and what profit shall this birthright do to me?" Although the threat of death seemed great to him, it is probably true that he also looked to the future, and knowing that all die sometime, he saw no value in the birthright. He was intent on those things that brought gratification for the moment—he placed no value on that which was spiritual. As far as Esau was concerned, future blessings were intangible. He saw no need to cling to a blessing that could not be enjoyed at the moment. Only the present was a reality for Esau.

Esau was supplanted by Jacob, but Esau really deceived himself. There is no excuse for what he did. The divine commentary on his action is given in Hebrews 12:16,17: "Lest there be any fornicator, or profane person, as Esau, who for one morsel of meat sold his birthright. For ye know how that afterward, when he would have inherited the blessing, he was rejected: for he found no place of repentance, though he sought it carefully with tears."

Esau would not have died from hunger—his parents, and undoubtedly others, were there, and they would have taken care of him. This also indicates that his concern about death had as much to do with the future as it did with the present. As he reflected on the fact that he would die someday, he thought the promises to the seed of Abraham were useless to him. In effect, he said, "I cannot live on promises. Give me something to eat and drink now. Tomorrow I may die, and nothing else will matter then."

Many Christians today are also more concerned about the present than they are about the future. They live for today

only and are unconcerned about tomorrow. This was not true
of Moses. When he considered the future, he "refused to be
called the son of Pharaoh's daughter; choosing rather to
suffer affliction with the people of God, than to enjoy the
pleasures of sin for a season; esteeming the reproach of
Christ greater riches than the treasures in Egypt: for he had
respect unto the recompence of the reward" (Heb. 11:24-26).

How different Esau was from Abraham and Isaac—even
Jacob. Hebrews 11:13,14 says of Abraham and other men of
God: "These all died in faith, not having received the promises, but having seen them afar off, and were persuaded of
them, and embraced them, and confessed that they were
strangers and pilgrims on the earth. For they that say such
things declare plainly that they seek a country." This was
not true of Esau. He lived for the present, not the future.

Both Jacob and Esau were at fault in the sale of the birthright. Jacob was wrong because he bought something that
God had promised would eventually be his on the basis of
faith. Esau was wrong because he sold something that was
not really his to sell.

The Believer's Birthright

The believer today also has a birthright. It is not material
but spiritual. Romans 8:16,17 says, "The Spirit itself beareth
witness with our spirit, that we are the children of God: and if
children, then heirs; heirs of God, and joint-heirs with
Christ; if so be that we suffer with him, that we may be also
glorified together." In verse 32 of this same chapter we are
told, "He that spared not his own Son, but delivered him up
for us all, how shall he not with him also freely give us all
things?" From these verses we see that we are joint-heirs
with Christ; thus, we have a spiritual birthright, for we will
inherit spiritual blessings.

In the first chapter of Ephesians, the Apostle Paul emphasized that the Christian is blessed, chosen, predestinated
and accepted in Christ (vv. 3-7). Chapter 2 reminds us that
"even when we were dead in sins, [God] hath quickened us
together with Christ, (by grace ye are saved;) and hath
raised us up together, and made us sit together in heavenly
places in Christ Jesus" (vv. 5,6). We are seated with him so

we might walk with Him, serve Him and enter into spiritual warfare with Him.

Having received Jesus Christ as your Saviour, are you serving Him today? Are you involved in the spiritual warfare? Even the spiritual warfare is part of what we inherit because of our spiritual birthright. Even though you are a Christian, perhaps you are living only for the pleasures of the moment and want no part of a spiritual battle. If this is true, then you are like Esau, who despised his birthright and sold it for a bowl of stew. All we have here on earth is nothing but a bowl of stew in comparison to what we will have throughout all eternity.

In Old Testament times, the birthright belonged to the firstborn. Since Jesus Christ was "the firstborn from the dead" (Col. 1:18), the spiritual birthright belongs to Him. Having received Jesus Christ as Saviour, we become joint-heirs with Him and inherit the blessings of the spiritual birthright.

Colossians 1 tells us concerning Christ that "by him were all things created, that are in heaven, and that are in earth, visible and invisible, whether they be thrones, or dominions, or principalities, or powers: all things were created by him, and for him: and he is before all things, and by him all things consist. And he is the head of the body, the church: who is the beginning, the firstborn from the dead; that in all things he might have the preeminence. For it pleased the Father that in him should all fulness dwell" (vv. 16-19).

Colossians 2:9,10 says, "For in him dwelleth all the fulness of the Godhead bodily. And ye are complete in him, which is the head of all principality and power." We have everything in Christ Jesus—we are complete in Him.

Believers are told in Ephesians 1:22,23 that God "hath put all things under his [Christ's] feet, and gave him to be the head over all things to the church, which is his body, the fulness of him that filleth all in all.," He that fills the whole universe also fills every believer. In Christ Jesus we have this birthright.

It is important that we understand what is meant by being "in Christ." This expression refers to place, or position, in that everyone who receives Christ as Saviour is placed into the Body of Christ by the baptism of the Holy Spirit (I Cor.

12:13). Because our position is in Christ we are to be in union with Him—letting Him have control of our lives.

The believer's union with Christ is seen from the Apostle Paul's words in Galatians 2:20: "I am crucified with Christ: nevertheless I live; yet not I, but Christ liveth in me: and the life which I now live in the flesh I live by the faith of the Son of God, who loved me, and gave himself for me." Christ and the believer are united—Christ is the believer's life. The importance of Christ's being in the believer is seen from Colossians 1:27: "Christ in you, the hope of glory."

A Life of Faith

All of this refers to a life of faith. You cannot buy it as Jacob bought the birthright. Colossians 2:6 says, "As ye have therefore received Christ Jesus the Lord, so walk ye in him." How did we receive Christ? We received Him by faith. Therefore, we are to walk, or live the Christian life, by faith. We are to be "rooted and built up in him, and stablished in the faith" (v. 7). We need to appropriate what we have in Christ Jesus. Do you want to appropriate the blessings of your spiritual birthright? If so, "set your affection on things above, not on things on the earth. For ye are dead, and your life is hid with Christ in God. When Christ, who is our life, shall appear, then shall ye also appear with him in glory" (3:2-4). When we appear with Christ in glory, we will then fully possess all that He has for us.

Emphasizing this same truth, the Apostle John wrote: "Behold, what manner of love the Father hath bestowed upon us, that we should be called the sons of God: therefore the world knoweth us not, because it knew him not. Beloved, now are we the sons of God, and it doth not yet appear what we shall be: but we know that, when he shall appear, we shall be like him; for we shall see him as he is. And every man that hath this hope in him purifieth himself, even as he is pure" (I John 3:1-3).

We cannot buy that which is ours through union with the Lord Jesus Christ. It can only be appropriated through faith. Jacob desired the birthright and the accompanying blessings, but he failed to realize that these could be his only by faith. Because he used carnal methods in seeking the birthright, God had to discipline him to bring him into submission. It took Jacob 30 years to learn the lesson God had for him.

Esau's Attitude

After Esau had sold the birthright to Jacob and had finished eating and drinking, he "rose up, and went his way: thus Esau despised his birthright" (Gen. 25:34). The word "despise" means "to look down on with contempt or aversion." It also means "to regard as negligible, worthless or distasteful." Esau treated his birthright with contempt, and because he regarded it as nothing, he willingly sold it for temporary satisfaction.

What are you doing with the privileges you have as a result of being united with Christ? Do you regard as nothing and treat with contempt the blessings you have because you are a joint-heir with Christ? Part of the responsibility of this birthright is our ministry—taking the Gospel to all the world. It is our responsibility because we are in Christ—it is not an optional ministry.

The Scriptures refer to others besides Esau who despised God's provisions for them. The Israelites were promised the land of Canaan, but God's Word says, "Yea, they despised the pleasant land, they believed not his word: but murmured in their tents, and hearkened not unto the voice of the Lord. Therefore he lifted up his hand against them, to overthrow them in the wilderness" (Ps. 106:24-26). The Israelites were more concerned about the things of the flesh than about the things of the Spirit.

Not only did the Israelites despise the land, but they also despised the One who came to be their Messiah. The Book of Zechariah predicted their rejection of Christ: "If ye think good, give me my price; and if not, forbear. So they weighed for my price thirty pieces of silver. And the Lord said unto me, Cast it unto the potter: a goodly price that I was prised at of them. And I took the thirty pieces of silver, and cast them to the potter in the house of the Lord" (11:12,13). Judas betrayed the Lord and later threw down the money in the temple, but the religious leaders were responsible for this. They bargained to get rid of Christ for 30 pieces of silver. Just as Esau despised his birthright, they despised the blessing that could have come to them through the Messiah.

In the Gospel of Matthew we read of those who despised their invitation to the marriage feast. In chapter 22 Jesus told the parable: "The kingdom of heaven is like unto a certain king, which made a marriage for his son, and sent forth his servants to call them that were bidden to the wedding: and they would not come. Again, he sent forth other servants, saying, Tell them which are bidden, Behold, I have prepared my dinner: my oxen and my fatlings are killed, and all things are ready: come unto the marriage. But they made light of it, and went their ways, one to his farm, another to his merchandise: and the remnant took his servants, and entreated them spitefully, and slew them" (vv. 2-6). These "made light of" the invitation to the wedding feast. They regarded it as nothing—they despised it.

Have you despised God's invitation—especially His invitation for you to receive Christ as Saviour? If you have received Christ as Saviour, have you regarded as nothing His invitation to be a co-laborer with Him in a spiritual ministry here on earth? Those of us who know Him as Saviour will one day stand before Him to give an account for what we have done for Him. Second Corinthians 5:10 reminds every believer, "For we must all appear before the judgment seat of Christ; that every one may receive the things done in his body, according to that he hath done, whether it be good or bad."

Those who reject Jesus Christ as Saviour often look with contempt on the goodness of God. The Apostle Paul asked such unbelievers, "Despisest thou the riches of his goodness and forbearance and longsuffering; not knowing that the goodness of God leadeth thee to repentance?" (Rom. 2:4). The goodness, forbearance and long-suffering of God lead the unbeliever to repent of his sins and to receive Christ as Saviour. These attributes also cause the believer to change his mind about living for the world and lead him to begin living for the Lord.

We may be sure that our sins will find us out. God's Word assures us of this, and Jacob's life graphically portrayed this truth. As we carefully consider God's dealing with Jacob during the 30 years after he bought the birthright, we see the results of refusing to dare to walk with God. Jacob wanted

God's best, but his error was in thinking he could obtain it by carnal means.

The God of Jacob is a long-suffering God. Psalm 146:5 says, "Happy is he that hath the God of Jacob for his help, whose hope is in the Lord his God." God dealt with Jacob in long-suffering, and He deals with present-day believers in the same way. How thankful we can be that our God is the God of Jacob.

Chapter 5

The Stolen Blessing

One faithless act leads to another. Having schemed to secure the birthright, Jacob deceived his father in order to secure the blessing, which was a vital part of the birthright. Jacob needed not only the birthright from Esau but also the blessing from his father. One was of no value without the other.

Consider the birthright and blessing of present-day believers. Our birthright, as we have indicated, is that which we have through our union with Jesus Christ. Our blessing is that which we have through the Holy Spirit. All that Christ is and shares with us is made real to us by the Holy Spirit. Before Christ ascended to heaven, He promised, "All things that the Father hath are mine: therefore said I, that he [the Holy Spirit] shall take of mine, and shall shew it unto you" (John 16:15). The birthright is ours because we are in Christ, and the blessing is ours because the Holy Spirit takes the things of Christ and makes them ours as we dare to believe Him.

The key to the Holy Spirit's blessing us is our attitude toward Christ. The Lord Jesus said, "If any man thirst, let him come unto me, and drink" (7:37). Jacob thirsted for the blessing of God. He longed to have what God wanted him to have. However, Jacob's problem was how to get what God wanted him to have. Jacob failed in his attitude toward God because he did not believe God for the blessings he was to have. As we have seen from the words of Christ in John 7:37, His command to "drink" is a command to take by faith what He has made available for us. Faith is the basis for our receiving the blessing that goes along with our birthright in Christ.

36

Isaac's weakness led to a plot by Rebekah and Jacob that dishonored God. "It came to pass, that when Isaac was old, and his eyes were dim, so that could not see, he called Esau his eldest son, and said unto him, My son: and he said unto him, Behold, here am I. And he said, Behold now, I am old, I know not the day of my death: now therefore take, I pray thee, thy weapons, thy quiver and thy bow, and go out to the field, and take me some venison; and make me savoury meat, such as I love, and bring it to me, that I may eat; that my soul may bless thee before I die" (Gen. 27:1-4).

Isaac loved Esau very much. The Scripture gives us the reason for this love: "Isaac loved Esau, because he did eat of his venison" (25:28). In his old age, Isaac's love for Esau became more prominent. This love for Esau took such pre-eminence in Isaac's life that he made preparations to act in direct opposition to the divine counsel that he was to give the birthright blessing to the younger son rather than to the older. God had made it clear to Isaac and Rebekah that "the elder shall serve the younger" (v. 23). Isaac's physical eyes were dim, and so were his spiritual eyes. Esau had sold his birthright for a bowl of stew, and Isaac was about to give away the blessing for some venison. Just as there was no excuse for Esau's act, so there was no excuse for Isaac's.

Esau was quite willing to go along with his father's suggestion. Surely he also knew of the divine plan that the elder was to serve the younger. However, after pondering for some time his loss of the birthright because of Jacob's scheming, Esau was apparently willing to do anything to reclaim his birthright. This provides a good illustration of reformation without regeneration. Esau was trying to change things by what he did, but there was no indication that he had faith in God.

Rebekah's Counterplot

Although Esau was the favorite son of his father, Jacob was the favorite son of his mother. Isaac was making plans to pass the blessing on to his favorite son, but Rebekah was not about to have Jacob left out—especially since God had indicated the blessing was to be Jacob's. Rebekah devised a counterplot. Her intent was to preserve for Jacob what God had intended for him. Her motive was seemingly good. To her, it seemed that God's purpose was in danger. She felt she must prevent great harm from coming to God's declared purpose concerning Jacob.

Genesis 27:5-10 says, "And Rebekah heard when Isaac spake to Esau his son. And Esau went to the field to hunt for venison, and to bring it. And Rebekah spake unto Jacob her son, saying, Behold, I heard thy father speak unto Esau thy brother, saying, Bring me venison, and make me savoury meat, that I may eat, and bless thee before the Lord before my death. Now therefore, my son, obey my voice according to that which I command thee. Go now to the flock, and fetch me from thence two good kids of the goats; and I will make them savoury meat for thy father, such as he loveth: and thou shalt bring it to thy father, that he may eat, and that he may bless thee before his death."

Jacob had his doubts as to whether Isaac could be fooled, for he said, "Behold, Esau my brother is a hairy man, and I am a smooth man: my father peradventure will feel me, and I shall seem to him as a deceiver; and I shall bring a curse upon me, and not a blessing" (vv. 11,12). However, Rebekah counted the cost and told Jacob, "Upon me be thy curse, my son: only obey my voice, and go fetch me them" (v. 13). Rebekah was willing to suffer the curse herself if Isaac became wise to her plot.

Rebekah's sin was that she lacked faith in God's ability. She felt she had to help God accomplish His will. While the intended goal was legitimate, the means she used to accomplish it were not honoring to God. She thought God must be frustrated concerning His plan and, therefore, needed her help. In this regard, Rebekah was like Sarah. Because Sarah was unable to bear children, she suggested that Abraham produce a child through her maid, Hagar. Sarah wanted to help God. Rebekah had the same lack of faith in God's ability to fulfill His plan.

Some people say, "The Lord helps those who help themselves." This is not true. The truth is that God helps those who come to the end of themselves. What we need is patience to wait on God. He is able to do everything He has said He will do, and He will always do it on time. Even the Son of God Himself had to wait on the Father to fulfill His plan. The Father promised the Son, "Sit thou at my right hand, until I

make thine enemies thy footstool" (Ps. 110:1). From the
Scriptures we realize that such exaltation for the Son came
only after His humiliation. Philippians 2 tells us how Christ
willingly gave up the position He had with the Father and
came to earth to die on the cross. Because of His willing
humiliation, "God also hath highly exalted him, and given
him a name which is above every name: that at the name of
Jesus every knee should bow, of things in heaven, and
things in earth, and things under the earth; and that every
tongue should confess that Jesus Christ is Lord, to the glory
of God the Father" (vv. 9-11). But even the Son of God had to
wait.

Jacob and his mother knew very little about waiting for
God's time and God's way. They preferred their time and
their way. They had not yet learned to depend on God to
fulfill His own promises. Possibly Rebekah never learned
this, and it took at least 30 more years for Jacob to learn it.

Consider how much trouble could be averted if we would
learn to wait on God. It does not take a great mind to think of
ways God could have prevented Esau from actually getting
the blessing. God could have caused Isaac to really think
about what he was doing and to change his mind. God could
have done many things, but Rebekah did not have faith that
God's plan was going to work out without her help. She felt it
was up to her to devise a way to help God out of His dilemma.

Although Jacob hesitated to take part in his mother's plot,
he did not seem as concerned about the sinfulness of such an
act as he was about being caught. He was afraid his father
would touch him, and then he would "seem to him as a
deceiver" (Gen. 27:12). Doing something that would dishonor God did not trouble Jacob as much as the thought that
he might be caught in the act. Most people experience sorrow
over sin when their wrongdoing is discovered. However,
they are usually sorry they have been caught instead of
sorry that they have sinned against God.

Jacob was afraid that he might *seem* to be a deceiver, but
by taking part in the plot, he actually *was* a deceiver. He was
refusing to call his actions sin.

In Rebekah's and Jacob's plot we see their old natures
seeking to take advantage of the old natures of Isaac and
Esau. All of them were in the wrong, and each was seeking

his own good rather than God's will and purpose. God will
not bless what He has determined should not be blessed.
Rebekah and Jacob did not have faith to believe this. They
did not have enough faith to trust God to abort Isaac's plan
to bless Esau. God would have seen to it that His will was
performed. After all, it was God who would bless, even
though the blessing would be bestowed through a human
instrument. This incident shows us the seriousness of trying
to run ahead of the Lord.

As Rebekah's plot unfolded, Jacob's true nature was
revealed. Instead of shrinking back in horror from the sin of
deception, he occupied himself with thinking about the possible unpleasant consequences of the sin.

After Rebekah had assured Jacob that the curse would be
upon her if he were found out and had commanded him
again to get the two young goats, Jacob "went, and fetched,
and brought them to his mother: and his mother made
savoury meat, such as his father loved. And Rebekah took
goodly raiment of her eldest son Esau, which were with her
in the house, and put them upon Jacob her younger son: and
she put the skins of the kids of the goats upon his hands, and
upon the smooth of his neck: and she gave the savoury meat
and the bread, which she had prepared, into the hand of her
son Jacob" (vv. 14-17).

Who was more to blame—the mother or the son? Although
we are not able to stand as judges, it is evident that Rebekah
had received direct communication from God that Jacob was
going to receive the blessing (25:23). In light of this promise,
she should have had enough faith in God to realize His plan
would not be thwarted. Rebekah had reason to distrust her
husband—he had been willing to sacrifice her chastity to
save his own life—but she had no reason to distrust God.
Although neither Rebekah nor Jacob could be excused for
what they did, it seems that the greater responsibility was
Rebekah's because of her communication from God.

Sin Upon Sin

Once the plot was put into operation, Rebekah and Jacob
kept heaping one sin on another. Genesis 27:18-20 says of
Jacob that "he came unto his father, and said, My father:
and he said, Here am I; who art thou, my son? And Jacob

said unto his father, I am Esau thy firstborn; I have done according as thou badest me: arise, I pray thee, sit and eat of my venison, that thy soul may bless me. And Isaac said unto his son, How is it that thou hast found it so quickly, my son? And he said, Because the Lord thy God brought it to me."

One lie always leads to another lie. Jacob kept adding sins to his previous ones. First, he impersonated his brother. Second, he lied to his father when he said, "I am Esau." Finally, he even went so far as to bring the name of the Lord into his deceit, for he said, "Because the Lord thy God brought it to me." Jacob most probably did not anticipate all of his father's questions; therefore, he had to have quick answers, which caused him to get into deeper and deeper trouble with his lies.

We can be sure that the Devil was supplying him with answers and encouraging him even to invoke the name of God to make his deception seem plausible. In Psalm 1:1 we see the progression of sin: "Blessed is the man that walketh not in the counsel of the ungodly, nor standeth in the way of sinners, nor sitteth in the seat of the scornful." Notice the words "walketh . . . standeth . . . sitteth." How much we blame the Lord for things that are nothing but acts of the flesh—the reaping of what we have sown. How tragic it is when we blame the Lord for the works of the flesh.

As Jacob stood before his father, Isaac said, "Come near, I pray thee, that I may feel thee, my son, whether thou be my very son Esau or not. And Jacob went near unto Isaac his father; and he felt him, and said, The voice is Jacob's voice, but the hands are the hands of Esau. And he discerned him not, because his hands were hairy, as his brother Esau's hands: so he blessed him" (Gen. 27:21-23).

Jacob must have thought the scheme had worked. No doubt Rebekah was carefully listening to what was going on and also thought the plan had worked! The flesh prides itself on its achievements. But there were to be many sad results from the works of the flesh.

Isaac's lack of discernment was due partially to his reliance on feelings. He was blind, or nearly blind, and he needed to rely on his sense of touch, but he also relied too much on his emotions. He was seeking to bless Esau because of his love for him rather than acting in accordance with what God had said about the elder son's serving the younger. We, too, are often guilty of acting in accordance with the way we feel rather than in accordance with the Lord's commands.

After Isaac felt Jacob's hands, he said, "Art thou my very son Esau? And he said, I am. And he said, Bring it near to me, and I will eat of my son's venison, that my soul may bless thee. And he brought it near to him, and he did eat: and he brought him wine, and he drank" (vv. 24,25).

Deceived by a Kiss

Isaac then said to his son, "Come near now, and kiss me, my son. And he came near, and kissed him: and he smelled the smell of his raiment, and blessed him, and said, See, the smell of my son is as the smell of a field which the Lord hath blessed: therefore God give thee of the dew of heaven, and the fatness of the earth, and plenty of corn and wine: let people serve thee, and nations bow down to thee: be lord over thy brethren, and let thy mother's sons bow down to thee: cursed be every one that curseth thee, and blessed be he that blesseth thee" (Gen. 27:26-29).

A kiss was part of Jacob's deception of Isaac, even as a kiss was part of Judas's betrayal of Christ. Isaac was deceived, and he pronounced the blessing on Jacob, but it was a long time before the blessing was fulfilled in Jacob's life. Because he had to reap what he had sown before he was ready to receive the benefits, 30 years passed before Jacob realized the benefits of the blessing. Again we are reminded of the words, "Be not deceived; God is not mocked: for whatsoever a man soweth, that shall he also reap" (Gal. 6:7). Jacob had sown to the flesh, and he reaped the results. His brother wanted to murder him, he had to flee from his father's house, he never saw his mother again, Laban deceived him for 20 years, he had to sneak away from Laban, some of his sons were wicked, and his own heart was broken later because his sons sold Joseph into Egypt. Jacob had many lessons to learn because of his reliance on the flesh to obtain spiritual blessing.

Esau's Defeat

Jacob's deception had brought defeat to Esau. The Bible says, "And it came to pass, as soon as Isaac had made an end of blessing Jacob, and Jacob was yet scarce gone out from the presence of Isaac his father, that Esau his brother came in from his hunting. And he also had made savoury meat, and brought it unto his father, and said unto his father, Let my father arise, and eat of his son's venison, that thy soul may bless me. And Isaac his father said unto him, Who art thou? And he said, I am thy son, thy firstborn Esau" (Gen. 27:30-32).

Jacob was found out! God's Word warns, "Be sure your sin will find you out" (Num. 32:23). Although in some cases a person's sin is not evident for a long time, in Jacob's case it took only a short time. He was suddenly found out as the schemer. The Bible does not tell us how much Isaac knew about Rebekah's part in the scheming. Perhaps he later learned all the details, but Jacob was completely found out immediately.

We cannot escape from God's all-seeing eye. In Hebrews 2:3 the question is asked, "How shall we escape, if we neglect so great salvation?" This verse refers to Christians who have not only salvation but a *great* salvation. It is more than salvation from hell and a guarantee of a place in heaven. It is a salvation that also gives victory, abundant life and blessing while we are on earth. If we are viewing our salvation only as an escape from hell and neglecting its other aspects, we will not escape. The day is coming when every believer will give an account to Jesus Christ. Second Corinthians 5:10 assures us, "For we must all appear before the judgment seat of Christ; that every one may receive the things done in his body, according to that he hath done, whether it be good or bad." This does not have to do with salvation because only believers will stand before the Judgment Seat of Christ. Our salvation will have already been determined. This will be a judgment for rewards, based on what we have done in this life for Jesus Christ. There will be no escaping having to answer for neglecting the abundant salvation Christ has provided for us.

Isaac's Reaction

Notice how Isaac reacted after he realized he had been deceived: "Isaac trembled very exceedingly, and said, Who?

where is he that hath taken venison, and brought it me, and I have eaten of all before thou camest, and have blessed him? yea, and he shall be blessed" (Gen. 27:33). I believe this is the key verse concerning the life of Isaac. This was his turning point. Isaac "trembled very exceedingly." In horror Isaac suddenly realized how he had been pitting himself against God's express purpose and pronounced will. He realized how God had graciously overruled him in the wrong he had almost done. Isaac had great fear before God when he realized what had happened. Isaac was condemned in his own heart for what he had almost done. God did not condone Jacob's sin; nevertheless, He used it to awaken Isaac to his own need.

At last Isaac came to his senses, for he really knew it was God's purpose and plan to bless Jacob, not Esau. What Isaac said when he realized all of this was one of the most crucial statements of his entire life: "Yea, and he shall be blessed" (v. 33). Isaac had no thought at this time of changing the blessing from Jacob to Esau. Of this incident, Hebrews 11:20 says, "By faith Isaac blessed Jacob and Esau concerning things to come." When Isaac was suddenly faced with his great mistake in endeavoring to bless Esau, he at once returned to fellowship with God and declared that the blessing was to remain on Jacob. God omits any reference to Isaac's weakness in the New Testament, where it is simply recorded that "by faith Isaac blessed Jacob and Esau concerning things to come." How gracious God is!

The pronouncement of faith that Isaac made and that God honored in no way indicated God's sanction of the sins that had been committed by the entire family. All four were guilty of sin. Esau had sold his birthright, Jacob had schemed to get it, Rebekah had planned and schemed with Jacob to get the blessing, and Isaac wanted to give the blessing to Esau. However, God forgives when confession is made. Isaac's and Jacob's sins are not mentioned in Hebrews 11—God blotted out their sins. Genesis 27:33 indicates that Isaac apparently made things right with God immediately. However, it took Jacob many years to realize his wrong. Twenty years later God asked him what his name was and he said, "Jacob" (32:27). By admitting that his name was Jacob, he was admitting he was a schemer and a deceiver. Because he admitted his name and his character, God changed his name to Israel (see v. 28).

Esau probably never confessed his sins because the Scriptures refer to him as a "profane person" (Heb. 12:16). Neither do the Scriptures record whether or not Rebekah confessed her sin to the Lord, although quite possibly she did.

Esau's Reaction

Observe how Esau reacted to his father's statement that Jacob would keep the blessing: "When Esau heard the words of his father, he cried with a great and exceeding bitter cry, and said unto his father, Bless me, even me also, O my father" (Gen. 27:34). Isaac answered, "Thy brother came with subtilty, and hath taken away thy blessing" (v. 35). Esau retorted, "Is not he rightly named Jacob? for he hath supplanted me these two times: he took away my birthright; and, behold, now he hath taken away my blessing" (v. 36).

Esau was bitter toward his brother because he had taken advantage of him twice. Desperate to have something, Esau asked his father, "Hast thou not reserved a blessing for me?" (v. 36). Isaac answered, "Behold, I have made him thy lord, and all his brethren have I given to him for servants; and with corn and wine have I sustained him: and what shall I do now unto thee, my son?" (v. 37).

Esau became more desperate and said to his father, "Hast thou but one blessing, my father? bless me, even me also, O my father. And Esau lifted up his voice, and wept" (v. 38). Esau did not weep because he was concerned about spiritual values but because he could not change his father's mind. Hebrews 12:17 says of Esau, "For ye know how that afterward, when he would have inherited the blessing, he was rejected: for he found no place of repentance, though he sought it [the blessing] carefully with tears." Esau was not repenting of his sin. He was trying to get his father to repent, or change his mind, of having given the blessing to Jacob.

Isaac refused to change his mind, and he said to Esau, "Behold, thy dwelling shall be the fatness of the earth, and of the dew of heaven from above; and by thy sword shalt thou live, and shalt serve thy brother; and it shall come to pass when thou shalt have the dominion, that thou shalt break his yoke from off thy neck" (Gen. 27:39,40).

Esau was as much to blame for the loss of the birthright as Jacob was in securing it through deceit and cleverness. Had it not been for Esau's attitude toward his birthright, it would not have been as easy for Jacob to take it from him.

The Reaping Begins

Having lost the blessing, the Bible says that "Esau hated Jacob because of the blessing wherewith his father blessed him: and Esau said in his heart, The days of mourning for my father are at hand; then will I slay my brother Jacob" (Gen. 27:41). Esau thought his father would soon die, but this was not the case. Even though he was quite old when he gave the blessing to Jacob, Isaac lived for many more years. However, this did not deter Esau in his plan to kill Jacob.

Rebekah learned of Esau's plot: "These words of Esau her elder son were told to Rebekah: and she sent and called Jacob her younger son, and said unto him, Behold, thy brother Esau, as touching thee, doth comfort himself, purposing to kill thee. Now therefore, my son, obey my voice; and arise, flee thou to Laban my brother to Haran; and tarry with him a few days, until thy brother's fury turn away; until thy brother's anger turn away from thee, and he forget that which thou hast done to him: then I will send, and fetch thee from thence: why should I be deprived also of you both in one day?" (vv. 42-45).

Rebekah urged Jacob to flee to her brother and stay there until Esau forgot about the stolen blessing. Notice that Rebekah said to Jacob, "That which thou hast done to him" (v. 45). Jacob was guilty of stealing the blessing from Esau, but Rebekah had devised the plan. Rebekah schemed again and decided it would be best for Jacob to go to her brother's home to live until Esau forgot about his plot against Jacob.

Rebekah did not expect that Jacob would have to stay long with Laban, for she instructed Jacob, "Tarry with him a few days, until thy brother's fury turn away" (v. 44). Esau was apparently very temperamental, and Rebekah assumed that, even though he was so angry at the time, he would soon forget about the entire matter. Assuming that Esau would soon forget, Rebekah told Jacob, "Then I will send, and fetch thee from thence" (v. 45).

Rebekah did not realize all the sorrow that was to be

reaped because of what she and Jacob had sown. After she
sent Jacob away, she never saw him again. She died before
he was able to return. Rebekah did not realize all the
calamity that would come on her because of her disobedience
to God. Like Rebekah, we sometimes think we can escape
reaping what we have sown—but we may be sure that our
sins will find us out.

To make it possible for Jacob to leave home, Rebekah went
to Isaac with this excuse: "I am weary of my life because of
the daughters of Heth: if Jacob take a wife of the daughters
of Heth, such as these which are of the daughters of the land,
what good shall my life do me?" (v. 46). The descendants of
Heth were known as the Hittites. Earlier, Esau had married
two Hittite women, and this had caused much grief for Isaac
and Rebekah (26:34,35). Rebekah posed the problem to Isaac
and let him decide what Jacob should do. It was a legitimate
problem, but Rebekah used it as an excuse to help Jacob flee
from Esau's wrath.

The Bright Side

We have seen the gloomy side of Jacob's life—that which
resulted from his scheming. But there was also a bright side.
This involved God's working with him to bring him back
into fellowship. God had selected Jacob for a purpose, and
what He had begun He was going to finish.

God is never defeated or frustrated when He sets out to
accomplish His purpose. His ways of accomplishing His
plan are beyond our comprehension. We must say with the
Apostle Paul, "How fathomless the depths of God's resources, wisdom, and knowledge! How unsearchable His
decisions, and how mysterious His methods! For who has
ever understood the thoughts of the Lord, or has ever been
His adviser? Or who has ever advanced God anything to
have Him pay him back? For from Him everything comes,
through Him everything lives, and for Him everything
exists. Glory to Him forever! Amen" (Rom. 11:33-36,
Williams).

As we study Jacob's life in detail, we see that every time he
was made to reap the fruit of his plotting and crookedness,
God was bringing him one step closer to fellowship with
Himself. Jacob not only schemed to get his own way, but he

also ran ahead of God. He wanted the things of God, but he wanted them in his own way and in his own time.

If we learn nothing else from Jacob's life, we should learn the importance of waiting on God. We are to wait expectantly on Him to fulfill His will in His own time. Although Jacob had sinned against God in his scheming, God caused His grace to abound over all of Jacob's sin and folly. Romans 5:20 tells us, "Where sin abounded, grace did much more abound." Does this mean that we should sin so grace can abound? The Apostle Paul anticipated this question and answered, "God forbid. How shall we that are dead to sin, live any longer therein? Know ye not, that so many of us as were baptized into Jesus Christ were baptized into his death?" (6:2,3). Paul emphasized that "our old man is [was] crucified with him, that the body of sin might be destroyed, that henceforth we should not serve sin" (v. 6). Although the grace of God is more prominent when seen against the backdrop of sin, this is no excuse for the believer to sin. God never condones sin but makes provision for forgiveness and cleansing: "If we confess our sins, he is faithful and just to forgive us our sins, and to cleanse us from all unrighteousness" (I John 1:9).

Lessons From Jacob

Some extremely important lessons from Jacob's life need to be underscored. We learn from him that we should never do evil in order to produce good. We should never try to win victories for Christ through unworthy means.

From Jacob we also learn the validity of the scriptural principle that our sin will be found out. This message is written in every line of the story of Jacob's life. Whereas every member of the family was guilty of sin, more is recorded about how the sin affected Jacob than about how it affected the others. Jacob was God's man; so many details are given to show how God worked with him.

If one lesson from Jacob's life is emphasized more than others, it is that God is sovereign. It is futile to suppose that we can thwart God's program or purpose in any way. The Scriptures abound in evidence of this fact. Proverbs 19:21 says, "There are many devices in a man's heart; nevertheless the counsel of the Lord, that shall stand." The Book of

Proverbs also declares, "A man's heart deviseth his way: but the Lord directeth his steps" (16:9). Emphasizing the same truth, the psalmist said, "The Lord bringeth the counsel of the heathen to nought: he maketh the devices of the people of none effect. The counsel of the Lord standeth for ever, the thoughts of his heart to all generations" (Ps. 33:10,11).

God Himself exhorted, "Remember the former things of old: for I am God, and there is none else; I am God, and there is none like me, declaring the end from the beginning, and from ancient times the things that are not yet done, saying, My counsel shall stand, and I will do all my pleasure" (Isa. 46:9,10). This should lead us to say as did Jeremiah, "O Lord, I know that the way of man is not in himself: it is not in man that walketh to direct his steps" (Jer. 10:23). The New Testament says, "So then it is not of him that willeth, nor of him that runneth, but of God that sheweth mercy" (Rom. 9:16). Isaac had his own will, but it came to nothing. Esau sought his own way, but he failed. God showed mercy to Jacob because He had chosen him as His special vessel.

Chapter 6

Blessing and Reaping

After Rebekah's plea to Isaac that Jacob not be allowed to marry a Hittite woman, Jacob was sent away with Isaac's blessing. The Word of God says, "Isaac called Jacob, and blessed him, and charged him, and said unto him, Thou shalt not take a wife of the daughters of Canaan. Arise, go to Padan-aram, to the house of Bethuel thy mother's father; and take thee a wife from thence of the daughters of Laban thy mother's brother. And God Almighty bless thee, and make thee fruitful, and multiply thee, that thou mayest be a multitude of people; and give thee the blessing of Abraham, to thee, and to thy seed with thee; that thou mayest inherit the land wherein thou art a stranger, which God gave unto Abraham" (Gen. 28:1-4).

Isaac probably did not know that Esau had sworn to kill Jacob after Isaac's death. However, Isaac lived several years after this time, and nothing ever came of Esau's treacherous plot.

Rebekah and Isaac had one plan for Jacob, but God had quite another. God's ways are higher than our ways. While people are prone to point out another person's failures, God is concerned about bringing out what is best in him. God is able to discern the true yearning of the heart and to bring about its realization. Basically, Jacob's desires were for the things of God—he wanted spiritual blessing. God knew this, and He worked to bring out the best in Jacob, even though Jacob often ran ahead and used carnal methods to attain spiritual blessing.

Having blessed him, "Isaac sent away Jacob: and he went to Padan-aram unto Laban, son of Bethuel the Syrian, the brother of Rebekah, Jacob's and Esau's mother" (v. 5). Jacob

50

had some great surprises in store for him. While he believed
God and had a deep-seated faith, he knew little about the
ways of God for his life. Jacob had a restless faith, and it was
very difficult for him to wait on God to work out His will. Five
of the seven communications of God with Jacob involved
God's correcting Jacob and redirecting him into His will.
Abraham also had seven communications, but each involved
a forward step of faith for him. However, Jacob had to be
corrected and directed back to the pathway of God's will.
Although this correcting brought many difficult experiences
for Jacob, he grew spiritually as a result. Jacob's restless
faith was evident when he plotted to obtain the birthright
and later the blessing because he was unable to wait on God.
As a result, he had to flee for his life because of the wrath of
Esau.

Genesis 28:10 says that "Jacob went out from Beer-sheba,
and went toward Haran." On his way to Padan-aram, God
made His first move to restore the fellowship that had been
broken. God always does this. Even concerning salvation
this is true. Jesus Christ Himself said, "No man can come to
me, except the Father which hath sent me draw him: and I
will raise him up at the last day" (John 6:44). No one can be
saved apart from the Father's making the first move. So
also, God initiated the move to restore His fellowship with
Jacob.

Jacob's Dream

Jacob was enroute to his uncle's home. On his first night
away from home, God met him and dealt with him in a
special way. Jacob "lighted upon a certain place, and tarried
there all night, because the sun was set; and he took of the
stones of that place, and put them for his pillows, and lay
down in that place to sleep. And he dreamed, and behold a
ladder set up on the earth, and the top of it reached to heaven:
and behold the angels of God ascending and descending on
it. And, behold, the Lord stood above it, and said, I am the
Lord God of Abraham thy father, and the God of Isaac: the
land whereon thou liest, to thee will I give it, and to thy seed"
(Gen. 28:11-13). This was the second time God called Himself
"the God of Abraham," and it was the first time He referred
to Himself as "the God of Isaac."

God also promised Jacob, "Thy seed shall be as the dust of
the earth, and thou shalt spread abroad to the west, and to
the east, and to the north, and to the south: and in thee and in
thy seed shall all the families of the earth be blessed. And,
behold, I am with thee, and will keep thee in all places
whither thou goest, and will bring thee again into this land;
for I will not leave thee, until I have done that which I have
spoken to thee of" (vv. 14,15). What a wonderful revelation
God made to Jacob!

The Lord appeared to Jacob in great tenderness, for He
knew that beneath the surface Jacob really desired to please
Him. God sought to bridge the gulf that existed between
Jacob's thoughts of materialism and his concern for spiritual realities. Jacob began to learn the two sides of life:
reaping the fruit of sin and seeing the triumphs of divine
grace. Jacob reaped what he had sown in his scheming and
carnality, but God also satisfied his deep, inner longing for
spiritual reality.

As Jacob lay under the stars while away from home that
first night, he was alone with his own thoughts. No doubt he
reflected on all that had happened. Perhaps he asked himself, Was it really worthwhile? Will I ever return to claim the
birthright and blessing for which I schemed and that I suc-
cessfully obtained?

Then he dreamed of a ladder that was set on earth and
reached to heaven with the angels going up and down it.
Even this revealed the gulf between him and God at this
time. God was at the top of the ladder; Jacob was at the
bottom. However, in spite of the gulf that existed, there was
communication between him and God. The ladder reached
down to where he was—down to his deepest needs. Yet it also
reached up to the very presence of God. What a revelation of
God's mercy and loving compassion! God was molding
Jacob into what He wanted him to be. At the top of the ladder
was the God of Jacob's fathers—the God of Abraham and
Isaac—and He promised to give the land on which Jacob
was lying to him and his descendants.

The Personal God

On this first night away from home, Jacob received his
first direct message from God. In speaking to Jacob, seven

times God used the personal pronoun "I." First, He said, "I am," emphasizing His omnipresence (Gen 28:13). Second, referring to the land, God said, "To thee will I give it" (v. 13). Third, God assured Jacob, "I am with thee, and will keep thee" (v. 15). Fourth, God promised, "[I] will bring thee again into this land" (v. 15). Fifth, God told Jacob, "I will not leave thee" (v. 15). Sixth, God assured Jacob He would be with him "until I have done that which I have spoken to thee of" (v. 15). There were no conditions for Jacob to fulfill. There were no ifs or buts—it was all of grace. God had sovereignly willed what was to be done, and His will would not be defeated—even by Jacob's carnality.

When God appeared to Jacob, He gave him a fourfold assurance (see v. 15). He assured Jacob of His divine presence—"I am with thee." He gave him the assurance of divine protection—"I . . . will keep thee." There was the assurance of divine preservation—"I . . . will bring thee again into this land." Jacob was also assured of the divine promise—"I will not leave thee, until I have done that which I have spoken to thee of."

God revealed Himself and His sovereign purpose to Jacob. God emphasized that He was ever-present—that Jacob could never get out of His sight. Jacob was experiencing the spiritual principle that "all things work together for good to them that love God, to them who are the called according to his purpose" (Rom. 8:28).

Jacob's Eyes Are Opened

Jacob's inner eyes were suddenly opened, even as Paul prayed for the Ephesians: "That the God of our Lord Jesus Christ, the Father of glory, may give unto you the spirit of wisdom and revelation in the knowledge of him: the eyes of your understanding being enlightened; that ye may know what is the hope of his calling, and what the riches of the glory of his inheritance in the saints, and what is the exceeding greatness of his power to us-ward who believe, according to the working of his mighty power" (Eph. 1:17-19).

When Jacob's inner eyes were opened, he was filled with awe, for he saw his undeserved prosperity and the wonderful promise that his descendants would be a blessing to the whole world. This was too much for Jacob. Genesis 28:16

says, "And Jacob awaked out of his sleep, and he said, Surely the Lord is in this place; and I knew it not." Jacob suddenly realized that his whole life was open to God—that God had seen all of his sins. At the same time, Jacob saw God's mercy and grace revealed to him—God was continuing to work in his behalf.

When Jacob realized all of this, "he was afraid, and said, How dreadful is this place! this is none other but the house of God, and this is the gate of heaven" (v. 17). Notice that Jacob called it a "dreadful" place, even though he also referred to it as the "house of God" and the "gate of heaven."

This seems to be when Jacob experienced true conversion. One can know truth about God, as Jacob knew the truth, but not be identified with it. I, too, was reared in a godly home and knew much truth about God. I had learned the catechism and had been baptized, but it was not until five years later that I understood the truth of regeneration and received Christ as my Saviour.

Jacob's heart was not at home with God, as evidenced by the fact that he thought the house of God and the gate of heaven was a dreadful place. His attitude at that time is a great contrast to David's attitude when he confessed his sin and cried out to God, "Against thee, thee only, have I sinned, and done this evil in thy sight. . . . Hide thy face from my sins, and blot out all mine iniquities" (Ps. 51:4,9). Jacob did not make such statements to God, but on his first night away from home, he began to realize that God is a personal God. Jacob was surprised to find that heaven was really so near. No wonder he was afraid. God is not far off but immediately present. Jacob began to view life from a new perspective when he realized, "The Lord is in this place; and I knew it not" (Gen. 28:16).

God Knows All About Us

God's house and God's presence are not dreadful to the person who consistently has close communion with God. Nor does such a person fear the fact that God knows all about him. What is your first thought when you are reminded that God knows every detail of your life? Take time to meditate on Psalm 139, which records the psalmist's awareness of God's complete knowledge about every detail of his life.

The psalmist said, "O Lord, thou hast searched me, and known me. Thou knowest my downsitting and mine uprising, thou understandest my thought afar off. Thou compassest my path and my lying down, and art acquainted with all my ways. For there is not a word in my tongue, but, lo, O Lord, thou knowest it altogether" (vv. 1-4). The psalmist realized that God knew what he was going to say even before he said it. As he pondered this truth, he said, "Such knowledge is too wonderful for me; it is high, I cannot attain unto it" (v. 6). With his finite mind, the psalmist could not comprehend the omniscience of God.

The psalmist continued, "If I say, Surely the darkness shall cover me; even the night shall be light about me. Yea, the darkness hideth not from thee; but the night shineth as the day: the darkness and the light are both alike to thee.... I will praise thee; for I am fearfully and wonderfully made: marvellous are thy works; and that my soul knoweth right well" (vv. 11,12,14). The psalmist closed this beautiful psalm with this prayer: "Search me, O God, and know my heart: try me, and know my thoughts: and see if there be any wicked way in me, and lead me in the way everlasting" (vv. 23,24).

Are you willing to allow God to search your heart? Jacob suddenly realized that God knew all about him. God knew about his meanness, crookedness and scheming. But God also knew that deep within his heart he was longing for spiritual realities; therefore, He undertook to mold Jacob's life to the praise of His glory.

God knew every detail about Jacob's life, and He knows every detail about your life. He knows the good things, and He knows the ugly things. He knows when you are putting on a front—acting like you are something that you are really not. He knows whether or not you are genuine—how much of what you say is really the truth.

How wonderful it is to know, however, that in spite of our shortcomings God loves us and will bring out the best in us if we will yield our lives to Him. God knew Jacob's inner longing for spiritual realities, and He loved Jacob. Jacob was afraid when he suddenly recognized God's presence. Perfect love drives out fear, but fear precedes perfect love. God's holiness, followed by His love and grace, revealed Jacob's sin to him. God can also reveal to us exactly what we are.

When we see God in His holiness, love and grace, we will realize how sinful we really are.

In Genesis 27:12 Jacob said to his mother, "My father peradventure will feel me, and I shall seem to him as a deceiver." Jacob did not admit he was a deceiver at that time. But on his first night away from home, when he was fleeing for his life, Jacob saw the sinfulness of his scheming heart when he saw God in His holiness. Jacob realized that God knew he was a deceiver.

When we see ourselves as we really are, there will be dramatic results—even as there were when the Apostle Paul saw himself. "As he journeyed, he came near Damascus: and suddenly there shined round about him a light from heaven: and he fell to the earth, and heard a voice saying unto him, Saul, Saul, why persecutest thou me? And he said, Who art thou, Lord? And the Lord said, I am Jesus whom thou persecutest: it is hard for thee to kick against the pricks. And he trembling and astonished said, Lord, what wilt thou have me to do? And the Lord said unto him, Arise, and go into the city, and it shall be told thee what thou must do" (Acts 9:3-6). In effect, the Lord was saying to Saul, "I know all about you. I know that deep in your heart you are committed to doing what you believe is right. I know what you will be. I have searched you, Saul. Go into the city, and you will be told what you are to do."

Job also was a good man in the sight of God. However, there were certain things that neither he nor others realized concerning his life. God Himself described Job as "a perfect and an upright man" (Job 1:8). Job put God first in all that he did. However, after God was through dealing with him, Job said, "I have heard of thee by the hearing of the ear: but now mine eye seeth thee. Wherefore I abhor myself, and repent in dust and ashes" (42:5,6).

Jacob's Memorial and Vow

After Jacob's exclamation that the place where he was staying was the house of God and the gate of heaven, he "rose up early in the morning, and took the stone that he had put for his pillows, and set it up for a pillar, and poured oil upon the top of it. And he called the name of that place Beth-el" (Gen. 28:18,19). Jacob made a memorial to God because the place had suddenly become sacred—he had met God there. Have you met God? Where did you meet Him? When did you meet Him? Have you received Jesus Christ as your Saviour and yielded your life to Him to live through you as He pleases?

Then Jacob made a vow, saying, "If God will be with me, and will keep me in this way that I go, and will give me bread to eat, and raiment to put on, so that I come again to my father's house in peace; then shall the Lord be my God: and this stone, which I have set for a pillar, shall be God's house: and of all that thou shalt give me I will surely give the tenth unto thee" (vv. 20-22). Notice the conditions of Jacob's vow— "if God." God did not have any conditions in His promises to Jacob, but Jacob's heart was not yet at home in the presence of God. It is difficult to trust God completely and immediately when we have become accustomed to making our own plans and running our own lives. This was Jacob's problem. It was difficult to yield completely and say, "Lord, I will leave everything to You."

Jacob wanted God's partnership, but he sought God's blessing on the things he had planned and wanted to do. Jacob failed to comprehend God's character and grace; so he met God's grace with an if and made a miserable bargain about food, clothing and journeying mercies. Then—and only then—would God be his God. How often we follow in Jacob's steps. Instead of appropriating God's unfailing grace, we bargain with Him and make stipulations and conditions. We should beware, because God will hold us accountable for our bargains.

Jacob had not yet found his rightful place in the presence of God; therefore, God used further circumstances to chasten him and bring him to Himself. Hebrews 12:11 indicates that chastening in the believer's life brings forth "the peaceable fruit of righteousness unto them which are exercised thereby." The purpose of God's chastening is so that the believer will bear more fruit.

Jacob still measured God by himself and thought of God only as a partner—someone he could call alongside to help him. It was utterly impossible for Jacob to comprehend who God really was. Jacob's God was small because Jacob measured Him by his own standards.

How big is your God? Most of us limit God because we confine Him to our ways. Jacob had to learn that God would have no part of his scheming attitude.

From his dream, Jacob learned that God would not leave him until His work of grace was done in his life. When Jacob awoke, his real life was just beginning. During the next 20 years, Jacob was allowed to experience many things to bring him to the end of himself. He bargained with one who was his equal in bargaining—Laban. Each tried to outwit the other, and Jacob was finally brought to the end of himself.

God knows how and where to train His saints. Sometimes it takes many years. It took 40 years for Moses, 13 for Joseph and 21 for David before they were ready to do the work God had chosen for them.

Do we really comprehend who God is and what He wants to do through us? As a believer, do you realize that Jesus Christ Himself lives within you? Do you realize the significance of Paul's statement: "I am crucified with Christ: nevertheless I live; yet not I, but Christ liveth in me: and the life which I now live in the flesh I live by the faith [faithfulness] of the Son of God, who loved me, and gave himself for me" (Gal. 2:20)? Can you say with the Apostle Paul, "I press toward the mark for the prize of the high calling of God in Christ Jesus" (Phil. 3:14)?

Chapter 7

Twenty Years of Discipline

His experiences at Bethel began a new life for Jacob. After
he had established a memorial to God, "Jacob went on his
journey, and came into the land of the people of the east"
(Gen. 29:1). The phrase "Jacob went on his journey" is literally "Jacob lifted up his feet." Jacob probably traveled
quickly—as if walking on clouds.

Remember the day you received Christ as Saviour? Or the
day when you met God in a special way? Perhaps you made a
great decision or had a great victory. Didn't it seem as if you
were walking on a cloud? No doubt that is how Jacob felt
with his new outlook. The revelation of God's presence and
the assurance of blessing brought light and encouragement
to his heart.

Jacob was making a long journey. It was more than 400
miles, and he was making the entire journey absolutely
alone on foot through country he had never seen before.

Because God protected Jacob, he arrived without any
trouble at the place in Padan-aram where his uncle lived.
Jacob came to a well where some men were watering sheep.
He asked some of them where they were from, and they told
him they were from Haran. When Jacob asked if they knew
Laban, they replied that they did. They assured him that
Laban was well and said, "Behold, Rachel his daughter
cometh with the sheep" (v. 6). What a unique meeting! God
had promised Jacob He would be with him, and this meeting
with Rachel was not by chance or accident. This is the way
God also works in our lives. We may go a certain direction,
but we never get out of God's sight. All that happened to
Jacob was by divine appointment—there is no such thing as
chance as far as God is concerned.

Jacob had failed miserably because he did not ask God for guidance. However, even though a person fails, God remains faithful. As the Apostle Paul said in his letter to Timothy, "If we believe not, yet he abideth faithful: he cannot deny himself" (II Tim. 2:13).

When Abraham sent his servant to bring back a wife for Isaac, the servant prayed for God's guidance (see Gen. 24:12-14). The servant of Abraham depended on God for guidance, but there is no record that Jacob asked for such guidance.

When Jacob met Rachel, it was apparently love at first sight. "And it came to pass, when Jacob saw Rachel the daughter of Laban his mother's brother, and the sheep of Laban his mother's brother, that Jacob went near, and rolled the stone from the well's mouth, and watered the flock of Laban his mother's brother. And Jacob kissed Rachel, and lifted up his voice, and wept" (29:10,11).

Jacob told Rachel that her father, Laban, was his uncle. At once Rachel went to tell her father about Jacob. Then Laban "ran to meet him, and embraced him, and kissed him, and brought him to his house. And he told Laban all these things. And Laban said to him, Surely thou art my bone and my flesh" (vv. 13,14).

Laban invited Jacob to stay with him, and thus began 20 years of grueling discipline that eventually led to Jacob's complete transformation. Jacob had experienced an inner spiritual change, but his outward life also needed to be transformed. During the 20 years God subjected Jacob to hard discipline so that He could make him a worthy instrument. His life reminds us of Proverbs 13:15: "The way of transgressors is hard." In Jacob's life we also see the truth of Galatians 6:7: "Be not deceived; God is not mocked: for whatsoever a man soweth, that shall he also reap."

Why Laban?

Although it seems to people that God sometimes moves slowly in carrying out His plans, we can be assured that His working is absolutely sure. God's method for Jacob was to put him with a man who was more difficult, greedier, more crooked and more cunning than Jacob himself. God's plan was to let Jacob see in another person all that was hateful about himself.

God still uses this method. Sometimes He places us in a certain position so that we will realize that it is not His will for us. This has happened to me on numerous occasions. In my early years of ministry I thought I would like to teach the Bible in the classroom. For three months God allowed me to substitute for another teacher. The Lord gave me this experience to show me that the classroom was not His place for me.

God has many ways of showing us what our hearts are really like. Left to ourselves, we would usually choose pleasant living conditions and congenial people to work with. But God is more concerned with our spiritual growth than with our temporal comforts. He will not spare us discomforts or pain if it will eventually mean eternal profit for us. God's love for us is strong and faithful. He has a purpose for every believer, and He uses the circumstances of life to accomplish that purpose and to make the believer more fruitful (Rom. 8:28).

What a disaster it would have been for Jacob if he had been put with a nice, reasonable person instead of with Laban. Jacob probably would have become proud and therefore useless to God. Jacob had a longing for the things of God; so God worked patiently with Jacob to change him for His glory and to break him from the habits of his old life. Because God knows every detail of our lives, He knows the circumstances He needs to use to bring us to Himself.

Jacob wanted God's gifts, and this was one great difference between Jacob and Esau. Esau despised the things of God and did not care to have anything to do with them. On the other hand, Jacob wanted the blessings of God so badly that he even tried conniving to obtain them. Although Jacob's methods were not right, they at least demonstrated how desperate he was to obtain the blessings of God.

God purposed to train Jacob by having him live with Laban. These men were similar in many ways, but there was also a great difference between them. Jacob believed in God, whereas Laban apparently did not, as evidenced by the fact that we are later told of his idols. However, God did not allow Laban to bring harm to Jacob. Laban would have sent Jacob away with nothing, but God was in control of the situation, and He saw to it that Jacob received proper payment for his diligent work. Jacob must have been a hard worker, and God even blessed Laban because of Jacob. God wanted Jacob to have plenty, and He allowed Laban to have plenty also. When God undertakes for us, He always does the right thing.

God did the right thing for Jacob, and He will do the right thing for you also. Learn to trust God. I have been encouraged over and over again by Psalm 37:5: "Commit thy way unto the Lord; trust also in him; and he shall bring it to pass." I have gone to this verse hundreds of times, and God has proven Himself absolutely faithful to His wonderful promise. If we will commit our way to Him—if we will simply trust Him for it—He definitely will bring it to pass.

Jacob Endures

Jacob demonstrated great strength of character in not running away from God's discipline. It was not easy for Jacob, but he stayed with Laban until God decided he had had enough. This reminds us of I Corinthians 10:13: "There hath no temptation taken you but such as is common to man: but God is faithful, who will not suffer you to be tempted above that ye are able; but will with the temptation also make a way to escape, that ye may be able to bear it." It took 20 years for Jacob to learn his lesson so that God could allow him to leave Laban. Jacob had to work 14 years for his beloved wife Rachel, and then he worked six more years to gain possessions for himself.

We gain nothing by running away or by trying to avoid God's dealings with us. Let the Lord take control of your life. If He has to take you through some disciplinary action to make you what He wants you to be, let Him do so because of the many blessings that will result for you. We will be the losers if we interfere with God's discipline in our lives. It is possible that God could have accomplished His purpose with Jacob in a shorter time if Jacob had submitted to Him sooner. However, it took God 20 years to accomplish His purpose in Jacob's life.

During the 20 years that Jacob was with Laban, Jacob's behavior demonstrated nothing of his experience at Bethel. There did not seem to be any significant change in his life.

I was 20 years old when I received Jesus Christ as my Saviour, and as I look back now, I realize there were several years after that time when my life really did not evidence the change that had taken place inwardly. God had to work in my life, sometimes harshly, before I demonstrated my new spiritual life in my everyday living. It was hard at the time, but I thank Him for it today.

No Significant Differences

Jacob struggled to gain worldly possessions. He seemed more concerned with accumulating property than with glorifying the Lord. Although Jacob believed God and his uncle was apparently an unbeliever, it is difficult to see any differences between the two. Both were greatly concerned with the possessions of life.

In our materialistic age it is also difficult to tell the difference between the believer and the unbeliever. Many Christians are so materialistic that they will make any kind of business agreement that will bring them gain. Some even say, "I keep my religion out of my business dealings." That was exactly Jacob's problem. He had difficulty realizing that his relationship with God should permeate every area of his life.

Because Jacob failed to comprehend the ways of God, God did something for him in Haran to teach him a valuable lesson. God, in His patience, taught Jacob what man really is. In his uncle, Jacob learned to see himself as he really was. His uncle was a greater schemer and more cunning than he was.

Although at Haran Jacob acknowledged God's presence and faithfulness, he did nothing without a scheme or a plan of his own. It was a shame for Jacob to do some of the things recorded in Genesis 29—31. God would have brought him many blessings had he waited, but Jacob felt he needed to scheme and plot to make sure the blessings would be his. It became a contest between Jacob and Laban to see who could outscheme the other.

Forced to Honor the Firstborn

Genesis 29:16-28 reveals at length how Jacob reaped what he had sown—how God allowed him to suffer from deceit. In this way God was able to teach him that there is no good thing in the flesh. Jacob made arrangements with Laban to work seven years for him so he could marry his daughter Rachel. The seven years passed quickly, for "they seemed unto him but a few days, for the love he had to her [Rachel]" (v. 20). At the end of the seven years, Jacob went to Laban and asked for Rachel.

Laban had another daughter Leah, who was apparently not as beautiful as Rachel. In those days it was the custom for the bride to wear a veil that made it impossible to see her face. She was then given to her husband-to-be by her father. In his deceit, Laban gave Leah to Jacob instead of Rachel. Because Leah came to Jacob in the evening and was so heavily veiled, Jacob did not recognize her. Jacob discovered it was Leah only after the marriage had been finalized. The next morning, when Jacob discovered Laban had given Leah to him, he went to Laban and asked, "What is this thou hast done unto me? did not I serve with thee for Rachel? wherefore then hast thou beguiled me?" (v. 25).

Laban told Jacob, "It must not be so done in our country, to give the younger before the firstborn. Fulfil her week, and we will give thee this also for the service which thou shalt serve with me yet seven other years" (vv. 26,27). Jacob fulfilled the week of celebrating his marriage to Leah, and then he received Rachel as his wife. Jacob had been thoroughly cheated.

Back in his home country Jacob had refused to submit to God. He was now compelled to submit to a human master—he had to serve, not dominate. Jacob was the youngest at home, but he had dominated the others; so God taught him a lesson by allowing him to be dominated by Laban.

Earlier, Jacob had not respected the rights of the firstborn, for he had schemed to get the birthright and the blessing away from Esau. Now, because of Laban's deceit, Jacob had to submit to the rights of the firstborn. By being required to marry Leah, the firstborn, before he could marry Rachel, Jacob learned his lesson the hard way.

Jacob also learned the lesson about waiting on God. He had refused to wait on God's fulfillment of His promise that "the elder shall serve the younger" (25:23). Because he refused to wait for God to fulfill this promise in His own time, Jacob had to leave home to save his life. Because Jacob had such difficulty waiting on God, He taught him, through the incident with Leah and Rachel, the importance of waiting. He had to wait seven years for Rachel, and this in itself taught him many lessons in waiting. Although he most likely married Rachel a week after he married Leah, he still had to work another seven years for Rachel before he could receive any wages for himself—14 years of waiting before he began to accumulate possessions for himself. God has ways of teaching people how to wait.

Laban Schemes to Keep Jacob

After 14 years with Laban, Jacob had taken about all he could, and he asked to be released. "It came to pass, when Rachel had born Joseph, that Jacob said unto Laban, Send me away, that I may go unto mine own place, and to my country. Give me my wives and my children, for whom I have served thee, and let me go: for thou knowest my service which I have done thee" (Gen. 30:25,26). However, God was not through teaching Jacob some valuable lessons. Therefore, God allowed Laban to devise ways for keeping Jacob from returning to his homeland.

Laban said to Jacob, "I pray thee, if I have found favour in thine eyes, tarry: for I have learned by experience that the Lord hath blessed me for thy sake. And he said, Appoint me thy wages, and I will give it" (vv. 27,28). This was a remarkable confession by Laban. He realized that the blessing that had come to him was not due to his own superior scheming but because of God.

The same principle applies to our salvation. We are not saved because of things we do but because of what Jesus Christ has done for us. The Word of God says that Christ "is the propitiation [satisfaction] for our sins: and not for our's only, but also for the sins of the whole world" (I John 2:2). In the same chapter, the Apostle John wrote: "I write unto you, little children, because your sins are forgiven you for his name's sake" (v. 12). We are not saved from condemnation by any works we are able to do, but by receiving as Saviour the One who paid the penalty for our sins. God's Word assures us that "as many as received him, to them gave he power to become the sons of God, even to them that believe on his name" (John 1:12).

Jacob Schemes to Deceive Laban

When Laban told Jacob to name his wages, this gave Jacob another opportunity to scheme and gain more blessings by deceit. Jacob told Laban, "Thou shalt not give me any thing: if thou wilt do this thing for me, I will again feed and keep thy flock. I will pass through all thy flock to day, removing from thence all the speckled and spotted cattle, and all the brown cattle among the sheep, and the spotted and speckled among the goats: and of such shall be my hire" (Gen. 30:31,32).

Jacob's wages had been changed several times, and during the next six years Laban changed them several times more. At this time, Jacob at least gave God credit, for he told Laban, "It was little which thou hadst before I came, and it is now increased unto a multitude; and the Lord hath blessed thee since my coming" (v. 30). But Jacob took full advantage of the opportunity to scheme to deceive Laban out of his possessions.

Although Jacob schemed and plotted, God did not let him out of His sight—and even continued to bless him. How marvelous was God's patience with His unworthy servant! God must have seen much in Jacob because of all the years He spent in disciplining him, leading him, overruling his mistakes and forgiving his sins.

Nothing is comparable to the patience and mercy of God! When we honestly examine our lives, we are unable to understand how God can be so merciful. We say with David, "Thy mercy, O Lord, endureth for ever" (Ps. 138:8).

None but God could have persisted with such a person as Jacob. None but God would have undertaken such a task with such a person. But grace begins at the very lowest point—it takes a person where he is and deals with him according to God's love and purpose. Truly, God's grace is amazing.

When God was finally through with Jacob and had forgiven all of his sins, it is said of God, "He hath not beheld iniquity in Jacob, neither hath he seen perverseness in Israel: the Lord his God is with him, and the shout of a king is among them" (Num. 23:21). Consider the grace of God that is revealed in this statement: "He hath not beheld iniquity in

Jacob." The verse does not say that Jacob did not sin, but God had forgiven it all and had blotted it from His mind.

What a marvelous God we have! Take time to examine your heart before God and confess any sin that is in your life. God has promised to forgive our sins when we confess them to Him (I John 1:9). Clear the record with God so that there is no unconfessed sin in your life. Because Christ shed His blood to pay the penalty for sin, it is possible for God to blot out your sin. Jesus Christ is the Lamb of God who has taken away the sins of the world.

Chapter 8

Jacob's Departure From Haran

Jacob's years with Laban were years of testing. Because of Laban's deceit, Jacob had to work 14 years to obtain Rachel instead of seven. Jacob then wanted to return to his homeland, but Laban enticed him to stay by giving Jacob another opportunity to scheme for material possessions.

Jacob stayed another six years with Laban, and during that time the sons of Laban became very jealous of him. Jacob overheard Laban's sons saying, "Jacob hath taken away all that was our father's; and of that which was our father's hath he gotten all this glory" (Gen. 31:1). In addition, "Jacob beheld the countenance of Laban, and, behold, it was not toward him as before" (v. 2).

The world does not always like to see a believer prosper. God allowed Jacob to prosper because He loved him and saw that the basic desire of his heart was to please Him. But because of Jacob's prosperity, the sons of Laban were jealous of him, and even Laban himself changed his attitude toward Jacob.

Believers who do not prosper materially or financially should not be troubled about others who do. We are counseled in Psalm 37:7,8: "Rest in the Lord, and wait patiently for him: fret not thyself because of him who prospereth in his way, because of the man who bringeth wicked devices to pass. Cease from anger, and forsake wrath: fret not thyself in any wise to do evil."

After 20 years of silence, God communicated with Jacob and said to him, "Return unto the land of thy fathers, and to thy kindred; and I will be with thee" (Gen. 31:3). Jacob had endured 20 years of heartbreaking experiences, but he was becoming prosperous in this alien land. Lest he become satisfied and want to stay in the land, God appeared to him and commanded him to return to the land of his fathers. God assured Jacob that He would be with him—the same promise of protection God had given him previously.

Jacob had wanted to return to his country, as evidenced by his words six years earlier: "Send me away, that I may go unto mine own place, and to my country" (30:25). However, Jacob did not leave Laban until the Lord commanded, "Return unto the land of thy fathers" (31:3).

How to Know the Will of God

An inner desire alone is not sufficient to determine the will of God. I believe three factors are essential in determining the will of God. First, we must have an inner desire. Jacob had this, for he wanted to return to his homeland.

Second, the commands of God must be obeyed—the Word of God must agree in principle with the person's inner conviction. Jacob had the direct command of God that he should return to the land of his fathers.

Third, circumstances must agree—they must make the action possible. These three factors—an inner desire, a divine command and favorable circumstances—will all be in harmony when it is God's will that something should be done. If even one is not in agreement with the other two, then you should be very careful in making any move.

If you have an inner desire and a divine command but the circumstances are not favorable, perhaps the way is right but the time is wrong. However, if you have an inner desire and the circumstances seem right, but the principles of God's Word would be violated by the action, you can be certain that the way is not right.

Too many Christians are led entirely by circumstances and desires. We must learn to wait on God. We must learn to trust Him completely. Psalm 37:5 says, "Commit thy way unto the Lord; trust also in him; and he shall bring it to pass." The psalmist prayed, "Lead me, O Lord, in thy righteousness because of mine enemies; make thy way straight before my face" (5:8).

We must also remember that "whatsoever is not of faith is sin" (Rom. 14:23). Concerning the will of God, Arthur W. Pink has written: "If you are sincere and patient, and pray in

faith, then, in His own good time and way, He will most
certainly answer, either by removing the conviction or desire
from your heart, and arranging your circumstances in such
a manner that your way is blocked—and then you will know
His time for you to move has not arrived—or, by deepening
your conviction, so ordering your circumstances as [so] that
the way is opened up *without your doing anything yourself,*
and by speaking definitely through His written Word.
'Commit thy way unto the Lord, trust also in Him, and He
shall bring it to pass' (Psa. 37:5)" (*Gleanings in Genesis,* Vol.
II, p. 77).

Psalm 25 is a wonderful psalm to meditate on when you
are seeking God's will. When you are faced with a difficult
decision, you will find every verse of this psalm especially
precious. The first eight verses emphasize the importance of
being in right relationship to the Lord so He can speak to
you. Verse 9 is especially important: "The meek will he guide
in judgment: and the meek will he teach his way." The meek
person totally relies on God for everything.

Verse 12 of this psalm says, "What man is he that feareth
the Lord? him shall he teach in the way that he shall
choose." The word "fear" is not used here as it is commonly
used today. In this psalm it refers to a reverential trust that
also involves a hatred of evil. To be led of the Lord, we must
trust Him completely and hate being out of the will of God. If
we fear the Lord in this way, He will teach us the way we
should go.

The psalmist also said, "The secret of the Lord is with
them that fear him; and he will shew them his covenant.
Mine eyes are ever toward the Lord; for he shall pluck my feet
out of the net" (vv. 14,15). In these verses we see that God will
never fail to fulfill His part if man fulfills his part. The
believer's responsibility is seen in the psalmist's words:
"Mine eyes are ever toward the Lord" (v. 15). When this is
true of us, we may be assured of God's leading in our lives.

The believer whose "eyes are ever toward the Lord" will
obey Paul's exhortation: "I beseech you therefore, brethren,
by the mercies of God, that ye present your bodies a living
sacrifice, holy, acceptable unto God, which is your reasonable service. And be not conformed to this world: but be ye
transformed by the renewing of your mind, that ye may

prove what is that good, and acceptable, and perfect, will of God" (Rom. 12:1,2). We must do this before we can ever know the will of God. We must totally commit ourselves—and everything about us—to God. He is not going to show us His will if we are not totally committed to Him. We become transformed by the renewing of our minds as we yield our minds totally to Him. When we do this, we will prove "what is that good, and acceptable, and perfect, will of God" (v. 2).

God's Time for Jacob

The circumstances were favorable for Jacob's departure. However, if Jacob had left Haran only because of the circumstances of personal hurt and resentment that he had earlier, he would have sinned. Many times we make this mistake. Our circumstances are difficult—perhaps people are talking about us, or we are unable to get along with our employer, our pastor or the people we work with. In such adverse circumstances it is easy to feel that God is telling us to move elsewhere, but if we move without God's direct appointment, we may find ourselves in far greater trouble.

In the record of Jacob's 20 years with Laban, there is not one mention of an altar at which he could commune with God. He may have had some inner communion with God, but the kind of communion associated with an altar—the special place of fellowship—was completely missing.

After God had made it clear to Jacob that He wanted him to leave Haran for Canaan, Jacob talked with his family. The Word of God says that "Jacob sent and called Rachel and Leah to the field unto his flock" (Gen. 31:4). He called them to a place where he could talk to them without being overheard. He had a scheme. He said to them, "I see your father's countenance, that it is not toward me as before; but the God of my father hath been with me. And ye know that with all my power I have served your father. And your father hath deceived me, and changed my wages ten times; but God suffered him not to hurt me" (vv. 5-7). Jacob told his wives some of the details of the way their father had dealt with him and how God had commanded him to return to his own land.

Having been cheated by Laban, Jacob learned by experience the kind of person he himself was and how his behavior had affected others. God uses this kind of lesson to teach us also. Perhaps we have been guilty of speaking against someone and have not realized how it may have hurt them. Then when someone speaks against us, we suddenly realize how deeply such words hurt, and we become sensitive to what we have done.

Even though Laban had deceived Jacob in the bargains they had made, Jacob prospered. Jacob told his wives that God had appeared to him and had said, "I am the God of Beth-el, where thou anointedst the pillar, and where thou vowedst a vow unto me: now arise, get thee out from this land, and return unto the land of thy kindred" (v. 13).

Because Jacob possibly had even more possessions than Laban, some might ask, Was God partial and biased? No, because God knew Jacob's heart. It cannot be emphasized too strongly that God knows the desires of our hearts. If you have been mistreated, cheated or deceived and if your heart has been right all along, be assured that God knows this. God will eventually vindicate you, but in the meantime you should be confidently aware that God knows the truth concerning what has happened to you. He knows if your heart has been right.

Rachel and Leah told Jacob, "Whatsoever God hath said unto thee, do" (v. 16). Once they agreed to leave with him, Jacob plotted how to flee from Laban.

Jacob Flees

Jacob waited for the right time to leave Laban. That right moment came when Laban had gone away from home to shear sheep (Gen. 31:19-22).

Before Rachel fled, she "had stolen the images that were her father's" (v. 19). Laban still had images—he was an idol worshiper. When Rachel stole these gods, she probably was not planning to use them, but she might have wanted to prevent her father from inquiring of the gods where Jacob and his household had fled. Perhaps Laban suddenly missed his gods because he was going to consult them when he learned that Jacob had fled.

There is another reason why Laban would have been greatly concerned about the missing household gods. According to the custom of the time, a son-in-law who possessed the household gods of the father-in-law could make a legal claim on the father-in-law's estate.

The Israelites worshiped idols and the false gods they represented only when they turned away from Jehovah. Many who claim to be Christians today have apostatized, for they have turned from the Bible to worshiping spirits, science and education. These people put their confidence in what man says rather than in what the Lord says.

Laban received the news "on the third day that Jacob was fled. And he took his brethren with him, and pursued after him seven days' journey; and they overtook him in the mount Gilead" (Gen. 31:22,23). Laban was seeking revenge, but he had to contend with One who was stronger than either himself or Jacob. "God came to Laban the Syrian in a dream by night, and said unto him, Take heed that thou speak not to Jacob neither good nor bad" (v. 24). God always watches over His own. He warned Laban not to harm Jacob.

We do not know how far Jacob had traveled by this time. Laban did not learn that Jacob had left until he had been gone for three days, and by the time he would have returned home another three days would undoubtedly have passed. Searching for his gods and preparing to pursue Jacob perhaps consumed another day. Then it took seven days for Laban to catch up with Jacob. So Jacob probably had been gone about 14 days by the time Laban caught up with him.

Laban overtook Jacob "in the mount Gilead" (v. 23). It is not certain where this was, but the land of Gilead was on the east side of Jordan. Two and a half tribes of Israelites occupied that area. Most likely the mount of Gilead was close to the border of the Promised Land. This is indicated also by the fact that it was not long after this that they crossed the brook Jabbok and entered into that part of the Promised Land.

Jacob Vindicates Himself

Laban said to Jacob, "Though thou wouldest needs be gone, because thou sore longedst after thy father's house, yet wherefore hast thou stolen my gods?" (Gen. 31:30). Immediately, Jacob felt he had to vindicate himself. He said, "With whomsoever thou findest thy gods, let him not live" (v. 32). Jacob was not aware that Rachel had stolen the idols.

Laban went from tent to tent looking for the gods. The Bible says, "Now Rachel had taken the images, and put them in the camel's furniture [saddle], and sat upon them. And Laban searched all the tent, but found them not. And she said to her father, Let it not displease my lord that I cannot rise up before thee; for the custom of women is upon me. And he searched, but found not the images" (vv. 34,35).

By this time Jacob was very angry. He said to Laban, "What is my trespass? what is my sin, that thou hast so hotly pursued after me? Whereas thou hast searched all my stuff, what hast thou found of all thy household stuff? set it here before my brethren and thy brethren, that they may judge betwixt us both" (vv. 36,37).

Then Jacob rehearsed some of Laban's injustices against him: "This twenty years have I been with thee; thy ewes and thy she goats have not cast their young, and the rams of thy flock have I not eaten. That which was torn of beasts I brought not unto thee; I bare the loss of it; of my hand didst thou require it, whether stolen by day, or stolen by night. Thus I was; in the day the drought consumed me, and the frost by night; and my sleep departed from mine eyes. Thus have I been twenty years in thy house; I served thee fourteen years for thy two daughters, and six years for thy cattle: and thou hast changed my wages ten times. Except the God of my father, the God of Abraham, and the fear of Isaac, had been with me, surely thou hadst sent me away now empty. God hath seen mine affliction and the labour of my hands, and rebuked thee yesternight" (vv. 38-42).

The believer has no such need to vindicate himself. Psalm 37:5,6 makes this clear: "Commit thy way unto the Lord; trust also in him; and he shall bring it to pass. And he shall bring forth thy righteousness as the light, and thy judgment as the noonday." God will take care of the believer, and He will vindicate him.

A Covenant of Separation

Because of their sharp disagreement, Laban suggested, "Let us make a covenant, I and thou, and let it be for a witness between me and thee" (Gen. 31:44). They gathered stones and heaped them together. Laban said, "This heap is a witness between me and thee this day. Therefore was the name of it called Galeed; and Mizpah; for he said, The Lord watch between me and thee, when we are absent one from another" (vv. 48,49).

This passage of Scripture is often used as a covenant of fellowship or a benediction. However, the context clearly indicates that it was not a covenant of fellowship but a covenant of separation. Laban said to Jacob, "This heap be witness, and this pillar be witness, that I will not pass over this heap to thee, and that thou shalt not pass over this heap and this pillar unto me, for harm" (v. 52).

This was the end result when two powerful schemers clashed with each other. They could not trust each other; so they had to make a covenant and set up a pillar of stones to mark the spot over which neither of them would cross for the purpose of harming the other. Each was really saying, "I cannot trust you out of my sight. The Lord must watch between us if we and our goods are to be safe from each other." Visiting between the families was not prohibited, but Jacob and Laban agreed never to cross the line for the purpose of harming the other.

After having sworn to the covenant, Jacob "offered sacrifice upon the mount, and called his brethren to eat bread: and they did eat bread, and tarried all night in the mount. And early in the morning Laban rose up, and kissed his sons and his daughters, and blessed them: and Laban departed, and returned unto his place" (vv. 54,55).

Chapter 9

The Carnal Man Becomes a Spiritual Man

Jacob the schemer arrived at his most critical moment—he had to face Esau, whom he had supplanted and cheated. Even more than that, he had to meet himself face to face and see how selfish he was. To do this, he had to come to the end of himself and see God as He really is.

After Jacob and Laban had made their covenant not to cross the boundary to harm each other, Laban returned to his place and "Jacob went on his way, and the angels of God met him. And when Jacob saw them, he said, This is God's host: and he called the name of that place Mahanaim" (Gen. 32:1,2). Jacob was finally free from his father-in-law, Laban, but he had a great danger ahead of him.

The Word of God tells us, "And Jacob sent messengers before him to Esau his brother unto the land of Seir, the country of Edom. And he commanded them, saying, Thus shall ye speak unto my lord Esau; Thy servant Jacob saith thus, I have sojourned with Laban, and stayed there until now: and I have oxen, and asses, flocks, and menservants, and womenservants: and I have sent to tell my lord, that I may find grace in thy sight. And the messengers returned to Jacob, saying, We came to thy brother Esau, and also he cometh to meet thee, and four hundred men with him" (Gen. 32:3-6).

God often has to bring us face to face with grave danger or a crisis before He can reveal His abundant strength to us. This was true also with the Israelites. When they were fleeing Egypt, they came to the Red Sea. The Red Sea was before them, the mountains were on one side, the desert was on the other side, and the Egyptians were behind them. What a critical moment! But in this crisis God appeared to the Israelites: "The angel of God, which went before the camp of Israel, removed and went behind them; and the pillar of the cloud went from before their face, and stood behind them: and it came between the camp of the Egyptians and the camp of Israel; and it was a cloud and darkness to them, but it gave light by night to these: so that the one came not near the other all the night" (Ex. 14:19,20). God brought darkness to the enemy and light to His own people—but it took a crisis for the Israelites to recognize the power of God.

As Jacob was now returning to Canaan and was face to face with his greatest crisis, the "angels of God met him" (Gen. 32:1). This was not the first time that angels appeared to him. That first night when he was fleeing from home, headed toward Haran, he saw a vision of a ladder with "the angels of God ascending and descending on it" (28:12). He also saw the Lord at that time, for He stood above the ladder and spoke to Him (vv. 13-15).

Jacob had also met the angel of God in Haran who reminded him of God's promise at Bethel and beckoned him to return to Canaan (31:11-13). When the angels of God met Jacob as he was returning to Canaan, he said, "This is God's host" (32:2). These angels came to welcome Jacob back and to escort and protect him as he entered the land. He had already been protected from Laban, and now they would protect him from Esau, who was coming with 400 men.

This situation is similar to that recorded in II Kings 6:13-17. Elisha and his servant were in the city of Dothan, and the enemy had surrounded it. When Elisha's servant saw all the horses and chariots of the enemy, he asked, "Alas, my master! how shall we do?" (v. 15). Elisha answered his servant, "Fear not: for they that be with us are more than they that be with them. And Elisha prayed, and said, Lord, I pray thee, open his eyes, that he may see. And the Lord opened the eyes of the young man; and he saw: and, behold, the mountain was full of horses and chariots of fire round about Elisha" (vv. 16,17). God was far more powerful than the enemy.

As Jacob was about to face Esau and his 400 men, it was comforting to know that the host of God was on his side. Jacob called the place "Mahanaim," which means "two camps."

Jacob Instructs His Messengers

As Jacob prepared to meet Esau, it was evident that he still had not grasped what it meant to really live by faith in God. Jacob still projected his own plans—he sent messengers to Esau and told them what to say: "Thus shall ye speak unto my lord Esau" (Gen. 32:4). How interesting that Jacob used the word "lord" in referring to Esau. After 20 years with Laban, Jacob had a different language. Before he had fled from his home, Jacob had lorded it over Esau and had taken away his birthright and blessing. But he now recognized Esau as lord. Humanly speaking, that was Esau's rightful place because he was the oldest. In referring to Esau as lord, Jacob was putting himself in the place of a servant. From the human standpoint that was his proper place because he was the younger of the two. God had promised that the blessing would go to Jacob, but it was necessary for Jacob to realize, as did the Apostle Paul, "By the grace of God I am what I am" (I Cor. 15:10).

Jacob instructed his messengers to tell Esau that he "sojourned with Laban, and stayed there until now" (Gen. 32:4). No reference was made to the fact that Jacob had fled from home earlier. Jacob had wronged Esau, and he could not have peace until he made things right with him. But nothing was said at this time about the wrong Jacob had done nor about his desire to make things right with Esau.

Jacob was apparently willing to forfeit the blessing he had taken from Esau by deceit. He wanted Esau to know that he was not returning to claim his birthright or that portion of his father's inheritance. In effect, Jacob was saying to Esau, "I already have enough; God has given me plenty."

Jacob had changed greatly in his 20 years with Laban, but the change was not sufficient to meet God's standards. Jacob was still far from being a mature believer. Jacob had grown during his 20 years with Laban, but he was not as mature as God desired him to be. In Hebrews 6:1 believers are told, "Therefore leaving the principles of the doctrine of Christ, let us go on unto perfection [maturity]; not laying again the foundation of repentance from dead works, and of faith toward God." Jacob had not progressed as much as God desired, but he did recognize Esau's rightful place as the elder brother and his own place as a servant. Although God would change this later, God had not yet permitted Jacob to benefit from the birthright or blessing he had obtained through deceit.

Jacob told his messengers to tell Esau, "I have sent to tell my lord, that I may find grace in thy sight" (Gen. 32:5). Jacob's message indicated that he recognized Esau's rightful place and that he himself was taking his rightful place, but the messengers returned with bad news. They reported, "We came to thy brother Esau, and also he cometh to meet thee, and four hundred men with him" (v. 6). Time had only intensified the hatred. Esau must have strutted with pride when he went to show his great power to Jacob. He had been beaten by Jacob's cunning, but he would let Jacob know that he now had the power to humble him. Esau's attitude was "I'll show him who's the better of us."

Jacob was in real trouble. What was he going to do? How often God has to bring us up against a wall of calamity before He can truly deal with our souls.

When Jacob learned that Esau was coming to meet him with 400 men, he "was greatly afraid and distressed: and he divided the people that was with him, and the flocks, and herds, and the camels, into two bands; and said, If Esau come to the one company, and smite it, then the other company which is left shall escape" (32:7,8). Jacob's first reaction was one of fear and distress; then he started making plans for survival. What about the angels who had met him? What about the promise God made at Bethel? "I am with thee, and will keep thee in all places whither thou goest, and will bring thee again into this land" (23:15). Jacob's reactions revealed his imperfect faith, and in this regard, he was like many of us.

Jacob's Prayer

Because of Jacob's imperfect faith, he offered a prayer of panic and then resorted to his carnal planning. In fact, Jacob began to plan even before he prayed. He took time out of his planning to pray, then immediately returned to his own schemes. He didn't seem to really trust God but only asked God to sanctify his plans.

How often we are guilty of the same thing. We pray as a

last resort. We do not have enough confidence to wait on God; we feel we must plot our own course if the work of God is to be salvaged. God has a perfect course of action for us to follow, and He can bless only as we follow His course. Paul said, "But none of these things move me, neither count I my life dear unto myself, so that I might finish my course with joy, and the ministry, which I have received of the Lord Jesus, to testify the gospel of the grace of God" (Acts 20:24).

When Jacob finally went to the Lord in prayer, his prayer evidenced the basic essentials of true prayer, but he lacked faith and true commitment. He came short of doing what the psalmist said we should do: "Commit thy way unto the Lord" (Ps. 37:5). But the psalmist did not stop there. He added, "Trust also in him; and he shall bring it to pass." Although Jacob did not have all of Scripture to guide him, he did have God's promise of protection.

When Jacob prayed, he said, "O God of my father Abraham, and God of my father Isaac, the Lord which saidst unto me, Return unto thy country, and to thy kindred, and I will deal well with thee" (Gen. 32:9). Jacob addressed his prayer to the God of a covenant relationship—the God of his fathers, Abraham and Isaac. Jacob appealed to God's faithfulness on the basis of His covenant with his fathers. This was very good. We, too, appeal to God the Father in the name of another. Our plea is based on our relationship to God, which has been made possible through our faith in the Lord Jesus Christ.

Jacob called on the God of his fathers, but he failed to call on God as his own God. He failed to appropriate what he knew about the God of his fathers. The faith he had was genuine, but he did not have complete faith in the promises of God. His faith was inadequate.

When you realize that the God of Abraham, Isaac and Jacob is your God, it should increase your faith. This is what Jacob failed to comprehend. He saw what had been accomplished in the lives of his fathers, but he failed to apply it to himself. He did not fully comprehend that the God of Abraham and Isaac was his God also.

Four elements of faith are extremely important: Faith believes that God *can* do what we ask; faith believes that God *will* do what we ask; faith *expects* an answer; and faith *accepts* the answer. The last point is crucial—unless we accept the answer, our faith falls short of what God intends it to be. This was Jacob's problem. He prayed and claimed the promises of God, but he did not accept the answer. He continued to scheme and to try to help God carry out His plan.

In his prayer Jacob referred to God as the One who said to him, "Return unto thy country, and to thy kindred, and I will deal well with thee" (v. 9). Jacob also recalled that God had said, "I will surely do thee good, and make thy seed as the sand of the sea, which cannot be numbered for multitude" (v. 12). Jacob was basing his prayer on the promises of God, and this is what God wants us to do. David prayed, "O Lord God, the word that thou hast spoken concerning thy servant, and concerning his house, establish it for ever, and do as thou hast said" (II Sam. 7:25). The believer is to claim God's promises and urge Him to "do as [He] hast said."

Concerning prayer, Philippians 4:6,7 says, "Be careful for nothing; but in every thing by prayer and supplication with thanksgiving let your requests be made known unto God. And the peace of God, which passeth all understanding, shall keep your hearts and minds through Christ Jesus." We are to expectantly ask God for the things He has burdened us to pray for. Our prayer and supplication is to be made "with thanksgiving." We are to say, in effect, "Thank You, Lord. I know You are going to answer. I accept the answer." The result of such a prayer is that God's peace, which passes all understanding, will keep our hearts and minds through Christ Jesus (see v. 7).

A Lack of Mature Faith

Jacob could have had this peace of mind. He could have said, "This situation is God's. He has promised to bring me back into the land, and He has sent his angels to take care of me. Thank You, Lord. I know You are going to take care of my brother, Esau." But Jacob did not pray in that way. Instead of committing the whole situation to God and saying, "Do as thou hast said," Jacob returned to his scheming to solve his problems.

This is a lesson all of us need to learn. As we pray for the salvation of our loved ones, we should not be overanxious

and expect God to work immediately. We are to allow God to
answer our prayers in His own time. It is not that God needs
a lot of time, but the people we are praying for may not be
ready. Or perhaps we ourselves are not ready. This is what
Jacob so badly needed to learn.

The Lord Jesus Christ told His followers, "What things
soever ye desire, when ye pray, believe that ye receive them,
and ye shall have them" (Mark 11:24). In I John 5:14,15 we
are told, "This is the confidence that we have in him, that, if
we ask any thing according to his will, he heareth us: and if
we know that he hear us, whatsoever we ask, we know that
we have the petitions that we desired of him." We must say,
"God, You said You were going to do it. I accept Your answer
now, but I leave the time to You." When we do this, the peace
of God will flood our hearts and minds.

Jacob's prayer was intense, earnest and good, but he
lacked the true or mature faith that would have accepted the
answer then and there. His prayer was also marked by
humility. Jacob said, "I am not worthy of the least of all the
mercies, and of all the truth, which thou hast shewed unto
thy servant; for with my staff I passed over this Jordan; and
now I am become two bands" (Gen. 32:10).

Jacob admitted his own unworthiness and God's mercy
and faithfulness. He accepted a lowly position before God.
This indicates that Jacob had come a long way in his spiritual life. God had worked in his heart.

It takes humility to receive the grace of God. James 4:6-10
says, "He gives us grace potent enough to meet this and
every other evil spirit, if we are humble enough to receive it.
That is why he says: God resisteth the proud, But giveth
grace to the humble. Be humble then before God. But resist
the devil and you'll find he'll run away from you. Come close
to God and he will come close to you. Realize that you have
sinned, and get your hands clean again. Realize that you
have been disloyal, and get your hearts made true once more.
As you come close to God you should be deeply sorry, you
should be grieved, you should even be in tears. Your laughter
will have to become mourning, your high spirits will have to
become heartfelt dejection. You will have to feel very small
in the sight of God before he will set you on your feet once
more" (Phillips).

As Jacob prayed, he said, "Deliver me, I pray thee, from the hand of my brother, from the hand of Esau: for I fear him, lest he will come and smite me, and the mother with the children" (Gen. 32:11). What was the motive for Jacob's petition? At first, it might seem selfish, but verse 12 indicates that Jacob was seeking the glory of God. Jacob was claiming God's promises when he said, "And thou saidst, I will surely do thee good, and make thy seed as the sand of the sea, which cannot be numbered for multitude."

We also need to check our motives when we are praying for the salvation of our loved ones. Are we praying for them only because they are loved ones, or are we truly concerned about the glory of God? Our chief concern should always be the glory of God. Whatever we do, we should "do all to the glory of God" (I Cor. 10:31).

Jacob still had fear, but it was an unnecessary fear. God had promised to bring him back to the land and to make his descendants as the sand of the sea.

The Rest of Faith

Jacob's faith—as evidenced by his prayer—was still very immature. Hebrews 11:1 says, "Faith is the substance of things hoped for, the evidence of things not seen." In reality, faith is having what you have asked for. But faith even goes beyond believing that you have what you have asked for—it produces something in your life. Hebrews 4:9,10 says, "There remaineth therefore a rest to the people of God. For he that is entered into his rest, he also hath ceased from his own works, as God did from his." This refers to the rest of faith. Faith rests in God and allows God to take care of the problems. When a person does this, he stops depending on his own works. But Jacob was not resting in faith—he was still trying to solve his own problems.

The rest of faith is vividly seen in the life of the Apostle Paul. He was on a ship that had been blown about by the wind for many days. It looked as if all the sailors and Paul would be killed by the storm. As Paul prayed during the night, God spoke to him. The next day he told the sailors, "I exhort you to be of good cheer: for there shall be no loss of any man's life among you, but of the ship" (Acts 27:22). How did Paul know that? How could he say so firmly that no one would die? Note Paul's reason for such assurance: "For there stood by me this night the angel of God, whose I am, and whom I serve, saying, Fear not, Paul; thou must be brought before Caesar: and, lo, God hath given thee all them that sail with thee. Wherefore, sirs, be of good cheer: for I believe God, that it shall be even as it was told me" (vv. 23-25).

What a tremendous encouragement this passage is! How different it is from the passages about Jacob. He prayed and told God all about his difficulty, but then he immediately began to scheme again. He could not believe, as did Paul: "I believe God, that it shall be even as it was told me." Jacob could have demonstrated the same faith because he had the same God. The promises of God were just as sure for him as they were for Paul.

Jacob had learned much during the 20 years he had spent with Laban, but his independent attitude still stood in his way. Reliance on self kept him from resting his faith completely in God. He was still a schemer.

A Plot to Appease

Genesis 32:13 tells how Jacob returned to his scheming immediately after praying: "And he lodged there that same night; and took of that which came to his hand a present for Esau his brother." Instead of trusting in God alone, Jacob plotted how he could appease Esau by giving of his possessions. Jacob substituted appeasement for deception. This perhaps shows some improvement, but his motives were still fleshly and debased in view of all the promises God had given him.

Jacob divided his livestock into several droves, "and he delivered them into the hand of his servants, every drove by themselves; and said unto his servants, Pass over before me, and put a space betwixt drove and drove. And he commanded the foremost, saying, When Esau my brother meeteth thee, and asketh thee, saying, Whose art thou? and whither goest thou? and whose are these before thee? Then thou shalt say, They be thy servant Jacob's; it is a present sent unto my lord Esau: and, behold, also he is behind us. And so commanded he the second, and the third, and all that followed the droves, saying, On this manner shall ye speak unto Esau, when ye find him" (vv. 16-19).

Jacob realized that his plan was not foolproof, for he said, "I will appease him with the present that goeth before me, and afterward I will see his face; peradventure he will accept of me" (v. 20). Jacob's plot of appeasement was an uncertain venture that resulted from his refusal to rely totally on the sure word of God. What a great enemy self is! Jacob lacked confidence in God to the extent that he actually distrusted God. Jacob plotted his own way because he did not have enough faith to believe that God could actually do what He had promised. Psalm 37:5 says, "Commit thy way unto the Lord; trust also in him; and he shall bring it to pass." Jacob had committed his way to the Lord, but he did not trust in Him; therefore, the Lord was not able to accomplish what He had promised. When we commit our way to the Lord and trust in Him, our burdens are placed on Him. Because Jacob did not trust the Lord as he should have, he continued to carry the burden himself. Jacob leaned on his own plan more than on God's sure word of promise. This is a vivid illustration of the works of the flesh. The flesh is always in conflict with the Spirit. Galatians 5:17 says, "For the flesh lusteth against the Spirit, and the Spirit against the flesh: and these are contrary the one to the other: so that ye cannot do the things that ye would."

When we are in the habit of thinking that we provide for ourselves, it is hard to trust God completely. We feel that somehow we have to help God if our needs are to be met. Instead of fitting into God's plan, we expect Him to bless our plans.

Jacob's plan was to appease Esau. The old nature wants to appease rather than face guilt. To be in fellowship with God, we have to face the guilt of our sins. Jacob was not willing to face and confess his guilt and to accept the judgment that God might mete out. The old nature, rather than seeking fellowship with God, seeks to advance its own desires by plotting its own course.

After Jacob had given instructions and the droves of animals had been sent off as presents for Esau, Jacob "lodged that night in the company. And he rose up that night, and took his two wives, and his two womenservants, and his eleven sons, and passed over the ford Jabbok. And he took them, and sent them over the brook, and sent over that he had. And Jacob was left alone" (Gen. 32:21-24).

Jacob still felt the outcome of the situation depended on him, so he did more planning and sent his family across the brook Jabbok for protection. It is admirable that Jacob made sure his loved ones were safe, but he was relying on his own plans for their safety instead of relying on the promises of God. God had sent His angels to protect them, but Jacob was unable to completely trust God to do what He had promised.

Jacob Is Left Alone

After Jacob's wives, women servants and sons had been sent over the brook, "Jacob was left alone" (Gen. 32:24). He remained outside the land of Canaan to guard against any harm that might come. God permitted Jacob to do this so He could deal with him while he was alone.

This introduces us to the most important crisis in Jacob's life. Some battles must be fought alone. There are times when no one can help us. This was just such a time in Jacob's life. Jacob's trouble was himself—his self-will, self-purpose, self-defense, self-desire and self-righteousness. Jacob's self-life had to be dealt with, and God chose to do so while Jacob was alone.

The Bible says, "Jacob was left alone; and there wrestled a man with him until the breaking of the day" (v. 24). This was a decisive night—it was the turning point in Jacob's life. He was alone with God, which is the only way of arriving at a true and just knowledge of ourselves and our ways. We must get away from the world, away from our selfish thoughts, away from our reasonings and imaginations—alone with God.

There are many scriptural examples of how God works with people when they are alone. For 40 years Moses was alone with God in the desert. God took him there to teach him many valuable lessons. When Moses came out of the desert, he was a different man. He could then trust God for everything and was therefore qualified to lead the Children of Israel out of Egypt. Without the great faith in God that he had acquired in the desert, Moses could never have accomplished this task.

David also realized the importance of being alone with

God. When David was living at Ziklag, he and his men were away from the city when the Amalekites invaded it and took the wives and children captive. The Bible says that "David was greatly distressed; for the people spake of stoning him, because the soul of all the people was grieved, every man for his sons and for his daughters: but David encouraged himself in the Lord his God" (I Sam. 30:6). David realized the importance of encouraging himself in God.

Jesus Himself made it a habit during His days on earth to spend time alone with His Father. If this was important for Him, it is much more important for us. Many things can be dealt with and decided only when we are alone with God.

The fact that Jacob was alone with God is the first key to understanding the change that took place in his life that night.

The Heavenly Wrestler

Jacob's plan was to stand guard against the possible night attack of his brother. He left nothing to chance; he did not sleep that night. This reveals his great concern for his family. As he stood watch, Jacob was suddenly attacked by a man who wrestled with him. Jacob was courageous and tried to conquer his foe. No doubt it was dark, and Jacob did not at first realize with whom he was wrestling. God had appeared in the form of a man and wrestled with him.

This passage of Scripture is often used to emphasize man's perseverance with God in prayer. However, we should observe that it was God, not Jacob, who began the wrestling match. Other passages of Scripture teach the importance of prevailing prayer, but it is not taught in this passage. Instead of persevering, Jacob was resisting continuously. He still felt competent to manage his own affairs apart from God, but the heavenly wrestler continued to struggle with him. This passage really teaches God's perseverance with His person until He can control him.

Jacob was not a coward, and because he had succeeded at almost everything he had attempted, it was natural for him to think that he could win this fight. It is a serious thing to resist God, whose only intent is to bless us. Jacob had to learn that he could never really gain the birthright, the blessing and the land of Canaan by his own cleverness.

They were to be received as gifts from God—by faith alone.

God's time for a confrontation had come. Jacob's most trying hour was ahead of him because Esau was coming with 400 men. This was a literal, physical struggle; yet in importance the physical was secondary to the spiritual. This is always true. This principle is seen in the life of the Apostle Paul, who had a thorn in the flesh and asked the Lord three times to take it from him. Paul wrote: "And he said unto me, My grace is sufficient for thee: for my strength is made perfect in weakness. Most gladly therefore will I rather glory in my infirmities, that the power of Christ may rest upon me. Therefore I take pleasure in infirmities, in reproaches, in necessities, in persecutions, in distresses for Christ's sake: for when I am weak, then am I strong" (II Cor. 12:9,10).

Jacob needed to learn that even though he was weak physically he could be strong spiritually. It took more than spiritual wrestling to convince Jacob of his need. God had been dealing with him spiritually for more than 20 years, but Jacob had failed to learn. God now struggled with Jacob physically because it was something Jacob could comprehend. Jacob's spiritual level of discernment was not mature enough for God to deal with him on a spiritual basis alone.

Sometimes God also has to deal with us on a physical level because this is the only thing that some of us really understand. It may involve the loss of wealth, health or family, but whatever it is, the loss is intended to draw us closer to the Lord. If we cannot be led spiritually, the Lord will communicate with us in a language we can understand. Let us become so sensitive to the Lord's leading that He will be able to deal with us purely on a spiritual basis.

Jacob Is Crippled

Genesis 32:25 says of the man who wrestled with Jacob, "And when he saw that he prevailed not against him, he touched the hollow of his thigh; and the hollow of Jacob's thigh was out of joint, as he wrestled with him." Because God was actually wrestling with Jacob, a question arises: Why couldn't He have prevailed without wrestling with Jacob all night? Certainly God could have brought Jacob to the breaking point sooner. But we should ask ourselves, How long has God had to wrestle with us? Because God is patient,

He has waited and worked with us for days, weeks, months and possibly years to bring us to the point where He wants us to be. How thankful we should be that God is so patient with us. Have you thanked God recently for His long-suffering and patience with you?

God wanted Jacob to come to the end of himself on his own. He gave Jacob every opportunity, but Jacob could not, or would not, break his self-will. Jacob experienced the long-suffering and patience of the Lord. The Word of God says that "the Lord is not slack concerning his promise, as some men count slackness; but is longsuffering to us-ward, not willing that any should perish, but that all should come to repentance" (II Pet. 3:9). Note especially that His long-suffering is directed toward us. The purpose of God's patient waiting is also stated in Isaiah 30:18: "Therefore will the Lord wait, that he may be gracious unto you, and therefore will he be exalted, that he may have mercy upon you: for the Lord is a God of judgment: blessed are all they that wait for him." The Lord waits so that He may be gracious to His children.

God knows just the right time to deal with His servant. The Lord had been waiting on Jacob for more than 20 years, but Jacob had not come to the end of himself. Now was the right time for God to directly confront His man. So the Lord appeared as a man to wrestle with Jacob. Even then He gave Jacob every opportunity to surrender, but Jacob would not. Jacob had rarely suffered defeat. But this time he was grappling with a different kind of foe—not a man, but God.

Because Jacob would not surrender, the divine wrestler dislocated Jacob's thigh and crippled him for life. This shows us the seriousness of resisting God.

Jacob had to be broken of his reliance on the flesh—the ways of the old nature. Jacob depended too much on himself and his own ability to accomplish what needed to be done. God had to touch his physical body to make him realize his need of depending on God. And God will have to do the same with us if we resist His working in our lives.

It is important for the Christian to recognize that the sentence of death must be passed on the flesh. Judicially, this has been done by the death of Christ, but we need to appropriate it by faith. Romans 6:6 says, "Knowing this,

that our old man is [was] crucified with him, that the body of
sin might be destroyed, that henceforth we should not serve
sin." This is what took place when Jesus Christ died on the
cross. But notice the need for our appropriation: "Likewise
reckon ye also yourselves to be dead indeed unto sin, but
alive unto God through Jesus Christ our Lord" (v. 11). We are
to reckon, or consider, it true because it is true. We are to
consider it a fact. Verses 12 and 13 say, "Let not sin therefore
reign in your mortal body, that ye should obey it in the lusts
thereof. Neither yield ye your members as instruments of
unrighteousness unto sin: but yield yourselves unto God, as
those that are alive from the dead, and your members as
instruments of righteousness unto God."

At the End of Self

The first key to God's victory in Jacob's life is that Jacob
was left alone with God. The second key is that Jacob had to
be brought to the end of himself. His own strength had to be
broken. He had come to the end of his own resources. All
confidence in his flesh had to be brought to an end, and this
was done when his opponent crippled him. Then he realized
his utter weakness.

Jacob could no longer fight his brother, Esau, in his own
strength, for his thigh was dislocated. Four hundred men
were coming with Esau, and Jacob was completely power-
less to do anything. Previously, he had resisted relying completely on the Lord, but now he had to because of his helplessness. He had to depend on God.

Because Jacob would not completely trust God's promises,
he had to learn that trust through total helplessness. God
had met him at Bethel and at Haran, and angels had met
him when he was returning to the land. But all of these
occurrences brought little response from Jacob. Therefore,
God had to resort to doing something Jacob would understand in order to bring Jacob to Himself.

What all must God do to us to bring us to the end of
ourselves? What must He do to us individually, organiza-
tionally, nationally and internationally to bring us to the
end of ourselves? We struggle, strive, fight and resist, but we
must realize that surrender to God is the only answer.

Self is the strongest internal antagonist we have to fight.

But we cannot overcome self by strength alone; in ourselves, we cannot conquer self. This is evident from Romans 7. The Apostle Paul wrote: "For I know that in me (that is, in my flesh,) dwelleth no good thing: for to will is present with me; but how to perform that which is good I find not. For the good that I would I do not: but the evil which I would not, that I do. Now if I do that I would not, it is no more I that do it, but sin that dwelleth in me" (vv. 18-20). In himself, the Apostle Paul did not have the strength to do what was right. In desperation he cried out, "O wretched man that I am! who shall deliver me from the body of this death?" (v. 24). But praise God, there is victory in Jesus Christ! Although we cannot overcome self in our own power, we are to recognize that "the law of the Spirit of life in Christ Jesus hath made me free from the law of sin and death" (8:2). That is why the old nature was crucified with Christ (6:6) and our relationship to it is as death. On our part, the victorious life is possible only as we have faith in God to accomplish this for us in practice. Therefore, we are to consider ourselves dead to the old nature but alive to God.

After the power of Jacob was broken because his thigh was dislocated, his entire attitude changed. As they wrestled, the angel of the Lord said to Jacob, "Let me go, for the day breaketh" (Gen. 32:26). Jacob answered, "I will not let thee go, except thou bless me" (v. 26). As the day dawned, Jacob no doubt realized who his assailant really was.

Jacob Clings to the Lord

At last God had Jacob where He wanted him, but what a tremendous cost it was to Jacob! No longer able to wrestle, Jacob began to cling. He changed from cunning to clinging and from resisting to resting. Jacob had at last begun to wait on the Lord and to rest in the promises of God. Hebrews 4:10 says that "he that is entered into his rest, he also hath ceased from his own works, as God did from his."

Jacob's clinging to the Lord is the third key to understanding the change in his life and walk. The first key is that Jacob was left alone, and the second is that the hollow of his thigh was dislocated. The third key is that his attitude changed from independence to dependence. Jacob began to cling for his life.

All that Jacob had struggled for he had lost; all that he had trusted God for he had gained. Like the Apostle Paul, Jacob realized that there was nothing good in his flesh. He realized that the only way out of his dilemma was God Himself. He was in the position to which God had been leading him for 20 years. In patience, God had waited until Jacob had come to the end of himself and had begun to cling to Him.

Jacob won more through this one solitary defeat than he had won through his many years of walking according to the flesh. But before the fullness of blessing could come, his strong self-will had to totally collapse. What was true of Jacob is also true of us—we must come to the end of ourselves.

Job was also an example of one who had to come to the end of himself before he could experience all that God intended for him. The first 31 chapters of the Book of Job show how Job grappled with his friends. He maintained his position against all of their arguments. He was a strong man; he stood for his rights. But chapters 32—37 record how God began to bring Job to the end of himself through the words of Elihu. Finally, beginning with the 38th chapter, God Himself wrestled with Job and completely overwhelmed him with the display of His greatness and glory. All of this caused Job to cry out, "I have heard of thee by the hearing of the ear: but now mine eye seeth thee. Wherefore I abhor myself, and repent in dust and ashes" (42:5,6).

We also need a new vision of the Lord Himself in all of His holiness, majesty and power. We will see God in His glory as we study the Bible, which is His revelation to us.

Jacob had stolen the blessing from Esau; now he was clinging to the Lord for His blessing. Jacob had contended with Esau and Laban and had succeeded. But when he contended with God, he utterly failed.

Before Jacob could receive God's blessing, he had to humble himself before God and confess his sin. It was necessary for him to face up to the sin and shame of his previous life. The angel of the Lord asked Jacob, "What is thy name?" (Gen. 32:27). Jacob's name had haunted him everywhere he had gone. His name presented him as a fraud, a sham, a cheat, a supplanter, a contender and a deceiver. When Jacob answered that his name was Jacob, he actually confessed to being all the things his name stood for. Jacob confessed the truth—his entire life was characterized by what his name represented. But when confession was made to God, he was at once on his way to receiving the blessing that God alone could give him.

From 'Jacob' to 'Israel'

The angel of the Lord told Jacob, "Thy name shall be called no more Jacob, but Israel: for as a prince hast thou power with God and with men, and hast prevailed" (Gen. 32:28). Jacob's name was changed, and he received royal blessings.

Jacob's new name, "Israel," means "prince of God" or "prince with God." This gave recognition to Jacob's new character. Although Jacob was no longer to be known as a deceiver, his old nature remained in conflict with the new nature, and occasionally the old nature gained prominence.

The name "Israel" indicated that Jacob was one whom God would command. Jacob was to be God's fighter and would no longer fight for himself. As Jacob had once prevailed for himself, under God's command and power, he would prevail for God.

Present-day believers are also engaged in a spiritual warfare. The Apostle Paul wrote: "Finally, my brethren, be strong in the Lord, and in the power of his might. Put on the whole armour of God, that ye may be able to stand against the wiles of the devil. For we wrestle not against flesh and blood, but against principalities, against powers, against the rulers of the darkness of this world, against spiritual wickedness in high places" (Eph. 6:10-12). When we identify ourselves with Christ in the spiritual warfare, we can say with the Apostle Paul, "I can do all things through Christ which strengtheneth me" (Phil. 4:13).

Jacob's plan to meet Esau had been perfected, but God took over. God took everything into His command, including Esau. It was no longer Jacob who was to arrange and order his life—it was God.

This was the third time God appeared to Jacob. The first time was at Bethel—the house of God—where God assured Jacob of His presence. Twenty years later, when Jacob was returning from Haran with his family and possessions, God appeared to him at Mahanaim, where the angelic host assured him of divine power and protection. The third time the Lord appeared to Jacob was at Peniel, where God brought Jacob into subjection.

Fellowship With God

These three appearances of God were progressive steps in the life of Jacob. First, he was assured of the presence of God. Second, he was assured of the power and protection of God. Third, he was assured of the favor and fellowship of God.

That Jacob had come into the presence of God for fellowship is evidenced by the fact that he called the name of the place "Peniel," for he said, "I have seen God face to face, and my life is preserved" (Gen. 32:30).

The believer's life of fellowship and friendship with God is his highest spiritual privilege. Although some use the expression "coming into the Lord's presence" when they pray, the believer is actually in the Lord's presence all the time. The believer is to always be walking in fellowship with God and conscious of His presence. The believer is also to make a practice of talking with the Lord at all times—he is not to wait until the end of the day to confess sin and bring requests to the Lord. He should be so sensitive to sin that he confesses it as soon as he commits it.

The believer's greatest privilege is that of constant fellowship with God. Concerning this fellowship, the Apostle John wrote: "That which we have seen and heard declare we unto you, that ye also may have fellowship with us: and truly our fellowship is with the Father, and with his Son Jesus Christ" (I John 1:3). Christ Himself said, "Henceforth I call you not servants; for the servant knoweth not what his lord doeth: but I have called you friends; for all things that I have heard of my Father I have made known unto you" (John 15:15).

Jacob finally came to recognize God as his Commander in Chief. The Scriptures tell of many others who had to come to this same realization. Joshua was such a person. He had taken over the leadership of Israel after Moses' death. The Israelites had crossed the Jordan River and were considering the conquest of Jericho.

"And it came to pass, when Joshua was by Jericho, that he lifted up his eyes and looked, and, behold, there stood a man

over against him with his sword drawn in his hand: and
Joshua went unto him, and said unto him, Art thou for us, or
for our adversaries? And he said, Nay; but as captain of the
host of the Lord am I now come. And Joshua fell on his face
to the earth, and did worship, and said unto him, What saith
my lord unto his servant? And the captain of the Lord's host
said unto Joshua, Loose thy shoe from off thy foot; for the
place whereon thou standest is holy. And Joshua did so"
(Josh. 5:13-15). Joshua recognized the Lord as his Commander in Chief, and as long as Joshua obeyed the orders of
God, he was victorious.

Isaiah's life was also changed when he "saw also the Lord
sitting upon a throne, high and lifted up" (Isa. 6:1). Seeing
God in all of His holiness caused Isaiah to be willing to say,
"Here am I; send me" (v. 8).

Others, too, were changed by a vision of God. Such was the
case with Jeremiah (Jer. 1:4-9), Daniel (Dan. 10:8-10) and
John (Rev. 1:13-19).

What a difference it makes when we see God in His fullness and walk in fellowship with Him. Do you know the Lord
in this way? It is the highest privilege you can have, but it
takes time and it requires seclusion. You will have to give up
self if you want to experience all that God wants you to have.

'The Sinew Which Shrank'

After Jacob's experience at Peniel, the Scriptures say that
"as he passed over Penuel the sun rose upon him, and he
halted upon his thigh. Therefore the children of Israel eat
not of the sinew which shrank, which is upon the hollow of
the thigh, unto this day: because he touched the hollow of
Jacob's thigh in the sinew that shrank" (Gen. 32:31,32).
Notice the beautiful expression "the sun rose upon him."
After Jacob had come to the end of himself and had settled
things with God, the sun rose on his life. Peniel was the
turning point in Jacob's life, for there he turned in another
direction. The fellowship that Jacob had with God as he left
Peniel was just as real as the sun that rose on him that day.
Jacob experienced a new, abundant life with God.

The present-day believer also has in his heart the Son of
God, who produces new life within. The Apostle Paul told of
the "mystery which hath been hid from ages and from gen-

erations, but now is made manifest to his saints: to whom God would make known what is the riches of the glory of this mystery among the Gentiles; which is Christ in you, the hope of glory" (Col. 1:26,27). What a wonderful truth it is for the believer to realize that the eternal God actually indwells him. Christ is our life. Our responsibility is to submit to Him so that He can live out His life through us. He will take charge of every aspect of our lives as we appropriate what He has made possible for us through His death and resurrection.

Genesis 32:31 says that Jacob "halted upon his thigh." He was now a broken man, and this brokenness was evident to all who saw him. Verse 32 refers to the "sinew which shrank." A doctor explained that the sinew of the thigh is the strongest part of the human body. If pulled straight out, a horse could hardly tear away the limb. Only by being twisted can it be disjointed, and in wrestling this is easily done.

The sinew was not removed from Jacob; rather, it shrank. I believe the sinew is representative of the flesh. It is impossible to remove or eradicate the flesh (Adamic nature) from the believer. Neither can the flesh be subdued; it must be withered. Its power must be broken and held in the place of death. Romans 6 makes it clear that the old man (flesh) has been crucified with Christ. Because the believer has died with Christ to the old nature, he is to live to God by the indwelling, resurrected Christ.

What Jacob had depended on for his strength had now shrunk to the extent that he was helpless—completely dependent on God. Jacob's old nature was not eradicated, for as he went to meet Esau and during the following years, it was evident that the old Jacob was still very much alive.

Jacob's new life was characterized by his new name, Israel. After Jacob's experience at Peniel, we see less and less of Jacob (the old nature) and more and more of Israel (the new nature). Jacob's attitude was now that expressed by John the Baptist, who said, "He must increase, but I must decrease" (John 3:30).

Chapter 10

After Peniel

After God changed his name, Jacob began to live a new life. But he learned very slowly. God is patient, but He is also firm. The conflict between Jacob's two natures became more prominent. In Jacob, God gives us a picture of the desperate struggle between the two natures that takes place in every believer's life. Jacob, in his conflict, was guilty of unbelief.

Unbelief is to be distinguished from disbelief. Those guilty of unbelief know the truth but do not obey it. They do not appropriate by faith what is available to meet their needs. This was the case with Jacob. He knew the truth but did not appropriate it. Disbelief, on the other hand, is true of those who simply do not believe the truth in the first place; therefore, they cannot appropriate it.

In recording Jacob's life, a typical biographer would emphasize the glowing victories that Jacob had after Peniel. The tendency would be to omit the failures that were due to his old nature. Jacob's name had been changed to Israel, but after Peniel, he is still referred to as Jacob many times in the Book of Genesis. It is also true that God called Himself "the God of Jacob," not "the God of Israel." If God had said, "I am the God of Israel," many of us would have difficulty depending on Him for our victories because we are too much like Jacob in his old nature. We need the God of Jacob. In effect, God said, "I am Jacob's God. I am willing to be called the God of any person if deep in his heart he yearns for Me. I will protect and guide that person to the end."

Others in the Scriptures had their names changed. Abram's name was changed to Abraham. Saul's name was changed to Paul. Simon's name was changed to Peter. With only a few exceptions in Peter's case, he was thereafter

referred to by his new name. This was not true of Jacob
because at first he acted more like Jacob than Israel. He
continued to supplant and deceive rather than to be commanded and ruled by God.

It is one thing to be privileged with a special vision, or
manifestation, of God, but it is quite another to live in the
power of it. This, however, is the privilege the present-day
believer has. Colossians 2:6,7 tells us, "As ye have therefore
received Christ Jesus the Lord, so walk ye in him: rooted and
built up in him, and stablished in the faith, as ye have been
taught, abounding therein with thanksgiving." Also, as we
are told in Ephesians 6:10, "Be strong in the Lord, and in the
power of his might."

Needless Fear

After Peniel there were four distinct steps of backsliding in
Jacob's life. The first was that of needless fear. Genesis
33:1,2 says, "And Jacob lifted up his eyes, and looked, and,
behold, Esau came, and with him four hundred men. And he
divided the children unto Leah, and unto Rachel, and unto
the two handmaids. And he put the handmaids and their
children foremost, and Leah and her children after, and
Rachel and Joseph hindermost [last of all]." Jacob had just
experienced a wonderful night with God that resulted in his
becoming the new man, Israel. But when he saw the
danger—Esau and his 400 men—fear gripped his heart.

Perhaps you say, "But it was only human for Jacob to
react this way." That is exactly the point. It was a human
reaction. God had assured Jacob that He would protect him;
so Jacob really had nothing to worry about. His name had
been changed to Israel, and he was to be God's fighter. God
was in complete charge of all circumstances, and Jacob was
to walk in that victory.

Jacob had already experienced how God could take care of
him when Laban caught up with him after he had fled. God
could also take care of Esau, but Jacob would have to bow to
God's control of the situation. Jacob was not to do the planning; he was to believe God and walk in the victory that God
would bring about.

The Christian who believes God is also assured of triumph
in the Lord Jesus Christ. Paul wrote to the Corinthian

believers: "Thanks be to God, which giveth us the victory through our Lord Jesus Christ. Therefore, my beloved brethren, be ye stedfast, unmoveable, always abounding in the work of the Lord, forasmuch as ye know that your labour is not in vain in the Lord" (I Cor. 15:57,58). God does not always remove the obstacles from our pathway, but He always gives power to triumph over them.

Jacob did not believe as he should have, but God was faithful because He could not deny Himself. God was in command even though Jacob did not believe. The Scriptures tell us, "If we believe not, yet he [God] abideth faithful: he cannot deny himself" (II Tim. 2:13). Jacob's life illustrates the truth of this verse.

Jacob was slow to appropriate and order his life according to the new name God had given him. But consider how slow we are to do the same. God calls us "saints"—this is what God has made us in His sight. He says in effect, "You can walk accordingly, and I will give you the strength to do so." God also calls us "sons." This is not something to be realized in the future; it is true now. The Scriptures say, "Beloved, now are we the sons of God" (I John 3:2).

God also calls us "heirs." Romans 8:17 says, "If children, then heirs; heirs of God, and joint-heirs with Christ; if so be that we suffer with him, that we may be also glorified together." God does everything for the believer. He indwells, empowers, commands, leads and fulfills—if we will but believe Him. The Christian life is a walk—it is lived a step at a time. The Christian life is not a magic carpet that suddenly transports us from one place to another. God provides all we need, but we must walk a step at a time.

Great experiences do not guarantee constant faithfulness. Jacob's experience at Peniel was a stepping-stone to greater living, but it did not guarantee faithfulness on his part. He had made significant progress during his 20 years with Laban, but he was not yet all that God intended him to be. Even Paul wrote: "Brethren, I count not myself to have apprehended: but this one thing I do, forgetting those things which are behind, and reaching forth unto those things which are before, I press toward the mark for the prize of the high calling of God in Christ Jesus" (Phil. 3:13,14).

Experiences that result from crises are like open doors that make it possible for us to enter a new aspect of our Christian walk. Thus, Jesus said, "If any man will come after me, let him deny himself, and take up his cross daily, and follow me" (Luke 9:23). We are to daily take our position in Christ and follow Him. Galatians 5:16 assures us that when we walk in the Spirit we will not fulfill the lust of the flesh. When we commit ourselves to following Him, the Holy Spirit controls our lives, and God lives His life through us.

Jacob Meets Esau

Jacob had tried to purchase Esau's favor earlier when he sent the various droves of animals out to meet him (Gen. 32:13-20). After his experience at Peniel, Jacob attempted to do the same thing again. We do not have to be cowardly before those who might harm us. We are to stand courageously with God. In the New Testament, believers are instructed to "put on the whole armour of God, that ye may be able to stand against the wiles of the devil" (Eph. 6:11). This same passage of Scripture exhorts, "Wherefore take unto you the whole armour of God, that ye may be able to withstand in the evil day, and having done all, to stand" (v. 13). We need to stand, not haughtily, but boldly in Him.

Jacob had earlier revealed that he was willing to take the place of the younger son before Esau when he referred to him as lord (Gen. 32:4,5,18). Now Jacob revealed this attitude again. Having divided his children and wives, Jacob "passed over before them, and bowed himself to the ground seven times, until he came near to his brother" (33:3).

When Jacob came near, "Esau ran to meet him, and embraced him, and fell on his neck, and kissed him: and they wept. And he lifted up his eyes, and saw the women and the children; and said, Who are those with thee? And he said, The children which God hath graciously given thy servant" (vv. 4,5). Jacob referred to himself as Esau's servant. He admitted that Esau was the oldest and that the birthright belonged to him.

It was no longer necessary for Jacob to fear Esau because God had everything under control—He even had control of Esau and Jacob. No one could harm God's chosen one. Even though people rebel against God, God's Word assures us,

"The king's heart is in the hand of the Lord, as the rivers of water: he turneth it whithersoever he will" (Prov. 21:1).

Jacob could finally say, as did the psalmist, "In God I will praise his word, in God I have put my trust; I will not fear what flesh can do unto me. . . . In God have I put my trust: I will not be afraid what man can do unto me" (Ps. 56:4,11). In Hebrews 13:5,6 is the same thought: "For he hath said, I will never leave thee, nor forsake thee. So that we may boldly say, The Lord is my helper, and I will not fear what man shall do unto me."

All of Jacob's planning was to no avail. God had subdued his enemy. Not only did God subdue Esau, but He also changed his heart attitude. What an unexpected reunion Jacob and Esau had. With this background, Psalm 46:7-10 is especially meaningful: "The Lord of hosts is with us; the God of Jacob is our refuge. Selah. Come, behold the works of the Lord, what desolations he hath made in the earth. He maketh wars to cease unto the end of the earth; he breaketh the bow, and cutteth the spear in sunder; he burneth the chariot in the fire. Be still, and know that I am God: I will be exalted among the heathen, I will be exalted in the earth."

Jacob Lies to His Brother

When Jacob and Esau met, Esau said, "Let us take our journey, and let us go, and I will go before thee" (Gen. 33:12). Esau offered to protect Jacob and those with him. Esau could easily have done this because 400 men were with him. But Jacob answered, "My lord knoweth that the children are tender, and the flocks and herds with young are with me: and if men should overdrive them one day, all the flock will die. Let my lord, I pray thee, pass over before his servant: and I will lead on softly, according as the cattle that goeth before me and the children be able to endure, until I come unto my lord unto Seir" (vv. 13,14). Jacob indicated he would meet Esau at Seir. But the account continues: "And Esau said, Let me now leave with thee some of the folk that are with me. And he said, What needeth it? let me find grace in the sight of my lord. So Esau returned that day on his way unto Seir. And Jacob journeyed to Succoth, and built him an house, and made booths for his cattle: therefore the name of the place is called Succoth" (vv. 15-17).

God had clearly instructed Jacob that he was to return to his father and to Bethel. Jacob knew this, but he failed to tell Esau he was following God's plan. Instead, Jacob led Esau to believe that he would follow him slowly and meet him in Seir. This was Jacob's second major step in backsliding after Peniel. Because of weakness and fear he lied to Esau. Jacob was afraid of what Esau might do, so he resorted to deceit. He feared Esau's temper more than God's disfavor.

Consider what Esau must have thought later when Jacob did not come as he had said he would. This supposedly spiritual leader lied to his brother because he did not have the courage to tell him he was following God. Words that are not supported by actions turn many people away from the Gospel. This is one reason the present-day church has lost rapport with the world. We are not direct in making our position with God known, and because of half-truths and timidity we are not winning people to the Lord as we should.

Jacob Stops Short

Jacob's third major step in backsliding after Peniel was that he did not completely obey what God had instructed him to do. He was to return to Bethel, but he stopped at Succoth. He stopped short of the perfect will of God—short of Bethel. Jacob sought earthly advantages just as Lot had. Perhaps the grazing at Bethel was not as good for his livestock, and perhaps the environment was not as good for his children. But whatever the reasons, he really had no excuse for disobeying God's instructions.

Jacob should have realized that seeking earthly advantages as Lot had done would only bring more trials. At Succoth, Jacob "built him an house" (Gen. 33:17). His tent life was temporarily abandoned. There is nothing sinful about a house or earthly possessions; it is our attitude toward material possessions that can constitute sin. God was not going to let Jacob rest until he arrived at the place where He wanted him. Thus, God caused Jacob to leave Succoth.

Farther, But Still Short

Genesis 33:18-20 says, "And Jacob came to Shalem, a city of Shechem, which is in the land of Canaan, when he came from Padan-aram; and pitched his tent before the city. And he bought a parcel of a field, where he had spread his tent, at the hand of the children of Hamor, Shechem's father, for an hundred pieces of money. And he erected there an altar, and called it El-elohe-Israel."

The word translated "Shalem" means "peace." Thus, the verse could read: "Jacob arrived safely and in peace at the city of Shechem." Although "Shalem" means "peace," Jacob did not have peace for long at that place. Again he purchased property so he could settle down. He was still short of returning to Bethel, even though perhaps he planned to return to Bethel later.

Jacob actually bought a piece of property that was his by promise. It was his by faith, but his faith was too small. Perhaps he reasoned that this was a good place to settle down to rear his growing family. In this place he saw all the advantages that made it attractive to settle there instead of returning to Bethel.

Jacob built an altar, but not where God had told him to build it. He was to have built it in Bethel, but in self-will he built it at Shechem. Many people are like this today. Attending church and having family devotions are very good things—and to be desired by all—but they are never substitutes for complete obedience.

I have heard some say, "I can serve the Lord here just as well as in some other place; there are many opportunities here." There are opportunities everywhere, but you cannot necessarily serve the Lord just as well in one place as in another. The only place where we can serve God as He intends is in the place to which He has called us. God's fullest blessing is found only in the place of His choice for us. Unfaithfulness in this regard will not be offset by attending church, by having family devotions or by any other activity.

Jacob called his altar "El-elohe-Israel." This name means "God, the God of Israel." No doubt Jacob was referring to himself and to the new name God had given him, because at this time there was no nation of Israel. Also, Jacob was probably referring to the vow he had made to God when he was fleeing from Esau: "If God will be with me, and will keep me in this way that I go, and will give me bread to eat, and raiment to put on, so that I come again to my father's house in peace; then shall the Lord be my God" (28:20,21). But neither Jacob nor the altar were where God ordered them to be.

Partial obedience is unsatisfactory to God. The account of King Saul vividly portrays what God thinks of partial obedience. Saul was to completely destroy the Amalekites and all of their possessions (I Sam. 15:3). However, Saul did not completely obey. He kept the best of the sheep and cattle and even spared the life of the king. When God, through Samuel, confronted Saul with his disobedience, Saul said, "The people spared the best of the sheep and of the oxen, to sacrifice unto the Lord thy God; and the rest we have utterly destroyed" (v. 15). Samuel said, "Hath the Lord as great delight in burnt-offerings and sacrifices, as in obeying the voice of the Lord? Behold, to obey is better than sacrifice, and to hearken than the fat of rams" (v. 22).

God did not accept Jacob's sacrifices and altar as long as Jacob was not in complete obedience. Let us learn this most important lesson. God is in command, and He expects total and unreserved obedience. Only then will He bless.

Jacob Reaps Through His Family

Jacob did not completely obey God, and he began to reap what he had sown, particularly in the lives of his children, for whose advantage he had probably settled in Shechem. One cannot stop short of God's will, purpose and place of service without reaping some bad fruit.

I believe this truth has a direct application to North America. Under God's hand this continent has enjoyed much protection and prosperity, but today even Christians are failing God and turning to materialism. God's hand of blessing and protection is thus being lifted. We are beginning to reap what we have sown.

The true Church is the restraining force against evil, but when believers become like the rest of the world, their restraint is nullified. Such Christians will also reap what they have sown. Too many Christians travel and move to places that will give their families mere material advantages without considering the proper environment of home, church, school and God's place of service for them. It has become the

custom for both the father and mother to be employed outside the home so that many children are reared by baby-
sitters. We may be sure that home life eventually affects
national life. As far as the believer is concerned, his home
life also affects his church life. Someone has said, "As goes
the home, so goes the church and the nation."

Many parents and pastors are in anguish of soul because
of the worldliness of their children. Such parents frequently
blame circumstances for what their children are like, even
though the circumstances were probably of the parents'
making. We must do more than blame the circumstances—
we must correct the situation. There was no progress in
Jacob's life until he corrected what he had done wrong.

How sad to realize that even Jacob's children experienced
the tragic effects of his unfaithfulness. Genesis 34:1 says,
"And Dinah the daughter of Leah, which she bare unto
Jacob, went out to see the daughters of the land." Dinah was
the only daughter, and I believe she may have felt the standards her parents had set for her were too restrictive. The
result was a debasing experience, for "when Shechem the
son of Hamor the Hivite, prince of the country, saw her, he
took her, and lay with her, and defiled her" (v. 2). Jacob was
reaping the results of incomplete obedience—his daughter
was defiled. What a heartbreaking experience this must
have been for Jacob.

In our day we have lost the concept of how desecrating and
defiling this sin really is. The New Testament gives us clear
instructions about defiling the body. First Corinthians
3:16,17 says, "Know ye not that ye are the temple of God, and
that the Spirit of God dwelleth in you? If any man defile the
temple of God, him shall God destroy; for the temple of God is
holy, which temple ye are." The sixth chapter of this same
book tells us, "Now the body is not for fornication, but for the
Lord; and the Lord for the body. . . . Know ye not that your
bodies are the members of Christ? shall I then take the
members of Christ, and make them the members of an harlot? God forbid. What? know ye not that he which is joined to
an harlot is one body? for two, saith he, shall be one flesh.
But he that is joined unto the Lord is one spirit. Flee fornication. Every sin that a man doeth is without the body; but he

that committeth fornication sinneth against his own body"
(vv. 13,15-18).

The sin of fornication is so serious for the believer because
it is committed against his body, which is a temple of the
Holy Spirit. The following two verses of this passage say,
"What? know ye not that your body is the temple of the Holy
Ghost which is in you, which ye have of God, and ye are not
your own? For ye are bought with a price: therefore glorify
God in your body, and in your spirit, which are God's."

A Satanic Suggestion

After Shechem had defiled Dinah, "his soul clave unto
Dinah the daughter of Jacob, and he loved the damsel, and
spake kindly unto the damsel. And Shechem spake unto his
father Hamor, saying, Get me this damsel to wife" (Gen.
34:3,4). Shechem tried to remedy the situation by offering
marriage. Observe that Satan, who brought about the fall of
man, suggested a remedy of mixed marriage—a believer
with an unbeliever. Verses 8-12 of this chapter tell how
Hamor presented the case for further coexistence with Jacob
and his people. Hamor said, "Make ye marriages with us,
and give your daughters unto us, and take our daughters
unto you" (v. 9).

Jacob had not come to this serious situation in one great
fall. By a series of steps he had come to this despicable
situation. First, he compromised. God had told him to go to
Bethel, which involved a separation from the world. Second,
he obeyed only partially. Jacob had gone only as far as
Shechem—there was not total separation. Third, this situation caused their only daughter to be tempted to investigate
the world around her. Fourth, she was defiled by Shechem,
the son of Hamor. Fifth, the Hivites offered to intermarry
and coexist with Jacob's family. Sixth, all of this led to
further sin within Jacob's own family.

The Bible says, "Jacob heard that he [Shechem] had
defiled Dinah his daughter: now his sons were with his cattle
in the field: and Jacob held his peace until they were come....
And the sons of Jacob came out of the field when they heard
it: and the men were grieved, and they were very wroth,
because he had wrought folly in Israel in lying with Jacob's
daughter; which thing ought not to be done" (vv. 5,7).

The Plot for Revenge

Jacob's sons plotted a way of revenge against Shechem and the Hivites. "The sons of Jacob answered Shechem and Hamor his father deceitfully, and said, because he had defiled Dinah their sister: and they said unto them, We cannot do this thing, to give our sister to one that is uncircumcised; for that were a reproach unto us: but in this will we consent unto you: if ye will be as we be, that every male of you be circumcised; then will we give our daughters unto you, and we will take your daughters to us, and we will dwell with you, and we will become one people. But if ye will not hearken unto us, to be circumcised; then will we take our daughter, and we will be gone" (Gen. 34:13-17).

In God's moral order He makes no allowance for compromise with evil. James 4:4 says, "Ye adulterers and adulteresses, know ye not that the friendship of the world is enmity with God? whosoever therefore will be a friend of the world is the enemy of God." Through the Apostle Paul, God also told us, "Be ye not unequally yoked together with unbelievers: for what fellowship hath righteousness with unrighteousness? and what communion hath light with darkness? And what concord hath Christ with Belial? or what part hath he that believeth with an infidel? And what agreement hath the temple of God with idols? for ye are the temple of the living God; as God hath said, I will dwell in them, and walk in them; and I will be their God, and they shall be my people. Wherefore come out from among them, and be ye separate, saith the Lord, and touch not the unclean thing; and I will receive you" (II Cor. 6:14-17).

God wanted the Israelites to possess the land of Canaan without compromising with the ungodly people around them, and today He wants the believer to live in the world but not to be a part of it. Coexistence with evil is in direct opposition to the principles of God. However, it has always been Satan's trick to get the believer to compromise with evil. Satan is gaining a great victory through the present-day emphasis on the ecumenical church. It offers so-called union at the expense of spiritual separation.

The sons of Jacob were deceitful. As was Jacob, so were his sons. Jacob was able to see himself in his sons. He could see the results of his own scheming. However, his sons went a step further by using a purely spiritual covenant to accomplish a worldly end that they felt was justifiable. They knew that what Shechem had done to their sister was a horrible sin, but what they plotted was not going to solve the problem.

Jacob's sons used a sacred covenant as a cover for premeditated murder. Their proposition "pleased Hamor, and Shechem Hamor's son" (Gen. 34:18). Hamor and Shechem went back to their people and urged them to consent to the proposal of Jacob's sons: "Hamor and Shechem his son came unto the gate of their city, and communed with the men of their city, saying, These men are peaceable with us; therefore let them dwell in the land, and trade therein; for the land, behold, it is large enough for them; let us take their daughters to us for wives, and let us give them our daughters. Only herein will the men consent unto us for to dwell with us, to be one people, if every male among us be circumcised, as they are circumcised. Shall not their cattle and their substance and every beast of their's be our's? only let us consent unto them, and they will dwell with us" (vv. 20-23).

Compromise always seems to bring gain. Lot entered Sodom for gain, and history has recorded the tragic results of his compromise. Genesis 34 proves to us that even unbelievers will compromise and agree to religious vows if they think they will profit.

Genesis 34:25-29 says, "And it came to pass on the third day, when they were sore, that two of the sons of Jacob, Simeon and Levi, Dinah's brethren, took each man his sword, and came upon the city boldly, and slew all the males. And they slew Hamor and Shechem his son with the edge of the sword, and took Dinah out of Shechem's house, and went out. The sons of Jacob came upon the slain, and spoiled the city, because they had defiled their sister. They took their sheep, and their oxen, and their asses, and that which was in the city, and that which was in the field, and all their wealth, and all their little ones, and their wives took they captive, and spoiled even all that was in the house." Such treachery in the name of religion! Some of the blackest crimes in history have been committed in the name of religion. When the Hivites were unable to defend themselves, they were killed.

Not only did the sons of Jacob commit murder, but they also ransacked the city, taking captive the children and the women and carrying off the wealth of the city. The women were perhaps put to use as slaves, and some possibly became wives of the captors. How cruel can men be? How far can they fall into sin? When a person is out of the will of God and compromises with the world, he may be surprised at the things he finds himself doing.

Jacob's Rebuke

Jacob did not take part in his sons' plot. However, he was reaping what he had sown. Finally, Jacob spoke up. He said to Simeon and Levi, "Ye have troubled me to make me to stink among the inhabitants of the land, among the Canaanites and the Perizzites: and I being few in number, they shall gather themselves together against me, and slay me; and I shall be destroyed, I and my house" (Gen. 34:30).

Jacob's rebuke was based on the human aftermath of what Simeon and Levi had done, not on the sin and dishonor their actions had been to God. All that Jacob seemed to be concerned about was what the people would do to him. Not only was Jacob overlooking the sin of his sons, but he was also completely forgetting God's promise to protect him and to bring him into the land again. God had told Jacob, "I am with thee, and will keep thee in all places whither thou goest, and will bring thee again into this land; for I will not leave thee, until I have done that which I have spoken to thee of" (28:15). When Jacob rebuked his sons, he was speaking as Jacob, not Israel. He was speaking as a supplanter and a deceiver, not as the prince of God.

Jacob had compromised. He had settled in Shechem, not Bethel. Now his old fears came back to haunt him. However, the Bible says, "There is no fear in love; but perfect love casteth out fear: because fear hath torment. He that feareth is not made perfect in love" (I John 4:18). Referring to Jesus Christ, Hebrews 2:14,15 tells us, "Forasmuch then as the children are partakers of flesh and blood, he also himself likewise took part of the same; that through death he might destroy him that had the power of death, that is, the devil; and deliver them who through fear of death were all their lifetime subject to bondage." God has overcome Satan;

therefore, we have no reason to fear if we are walking in fellowship with God. Jacob feared because he was not separated unto God and completely obedient to God's will. One begins to wonder how much more Jacob would have to endure before he would see his need of complete reliance on and obedience to God.

After Jacob rebuked his sons, they asked, "Should he deal with our sister as with an harlot?" (Gen. 34:31). Simeon and Levi tried to justify their actions. At times, do we not also think it is all right to do evil in order that good may result? Jacob's sons were right—Shechem never should have defiled their sister. And it would not have happened if Jacob had gone to Bethel as God had instructed him. Jacob compromised, and his sons compromised with him. The sin of Shechem was awful, but the sins of deceit and murder did not correct anything. One sin is not made right by committing another.

Jacob never forgot the deeds of his sons. Later he said, "Simeon and Levi are brethren; instruments of cruelty are in their habitations. O my soul, come not thou into their secret; unto their assembly, mine honour, be not thou united: for in their anger they slew a man, and in their selfwill they digged down a wall. Cursed be their anger, for it was fierce; and their wrath, for it was cruel: I will divide them in Jacob, and scatter them in Israel" (49:5-7).

Worldliness

The lesson that stands out from this incident is the danger of worldliness. Worldliness is hard to define, but it is easy to detect and describe. It is an atmosphere that is poisonous, deadening and disastrous to the soul, and it is *always* dishonoring to God. It leads to deeper and deeper sin. Worldliness prevents spiritual blessing. Jacob could have no testimony among the Gentiles where he lived because of his compromise and worldliness.

Both Abraham and Isaac were guilty of lying about their wives, but both of them made things right with God and brought honor to Him by the way they lived. As a result, they were respected by those around them. How different it was, however, with Lot in Sodom and with Jacob.

Worldliness can be prevented only by complete separation. Christ's prayer, recorded in John 17, revealed the only safeguard against the insidious peril of worldliness. First, as Christ prayed to the Father, He said, "I have manifested thy name unto the men which thou gavest me out of the world" (v. 6). God took them out of the world and gave them to Jesus. Second, Jesus said, "Now I am no more in the world, but these are in the world" (v. 11). Third, Christ said, "I have given them thy word; and the world hath hated them" (v. 14). Fourth, Christ said that the world hated them "because they are not of the world, even as I am not of the world" (v. 14). The believers were in the world, but they were not to be of the world. Fifth, Christ said, "I pray not that thou shouldest take them out of the world, but that thou shouldest keep them from the evil [one]" (v. 15). Sixth, Christ prayed, "As thou hast sent me into the world, even so have I also sent them into the world" (v. 18). Seventh, the reason Christ prayed that the believers would be sent into the world but kept from the world was so "the world may know that thou hast sent me, and hast loved them, as thou hast loved me" (v. 23). They were to witness *to* the world but not to be *of* the world.

Jacob Reaches the Bottom

God allowed Jacob to go to the depths of sin. Worldliness completely overwhelmed him. He could not have gone any lower, and his family could not have gone any lower. Their reputation among the people around them was destroyed. They were guilty of murder because of their desire to right a wrong against their family. Even though Jacob had fallen to the depths of sin, God never stopped working with him. God did not leave Jacob alone until he was back in the center of His will. God commanded him, "Arise, go up to Beth-el, and dwell there: and make there an altar unto God, that appeared unto thee when thou fleddest from the face of Esau thy brother" (Gen. 35:1). Even though Jacob often turned his back on God, God was never unfaithful to Jacob. It is wonderful to know that the God of Jacob is our God also. How long-suffering and merciful God is to His own! With Jeremiah, every believer can say, "It is of the Lord's mercies that we are not consumed, because his compassions fail not. They are new every morning: great is thy faithfulness" (Lam. 3:22,23).

Chapter 11

Bethel at Last

Jacob had spent 20 years with Laban under the disciplining hand of God. During this time, God was working with Jacob to make him the kind of man He wanted him to be. During those 20 years Jacob sowed both good and bad, and he reaped as he had sown. For the most part, however, his life during that time was lived in the energy of the flesh. Then, at Peniel, Jacob met God and had his name changed to Israel. Jacob knew the importance of returning to Bethel, but for 10 years after his experience at Peniel, he lived in a backslidden condition.

Just as Christ told the Church of Ephesus to "remember therefore from whence thou art fallen, and repent, and do the first works" (Rev. 2:5), so God instructed Jacob to return to Bethel. It was only about 30 miles from Shechem to Bethel, but Jacob stayed at Shechem for nearly 10 years. There he reaped what he had sown in the flesh. The way back to God is repentance and faith. The two always go together. Jacob was still not living in complete fellowship with God. Although he had been back in the land for 10 years, he was still short of Bethel. But at Shechem, God shut Jacob up to Himself.

Because of what his sons had done, Jacob needed to flee Shechem. But where could he go? He could not go back to Laban. Neither could he go back to Esau, for he had deceived him on the other side of the Jordan. Jacob had said he would follow slowly after Esau and meet him in Seir, but instead Jacob went to Succoth and then on to Shechem. God had Jacob where He wanted him. Jacob was hemmed in on all sides. He had no place to flee but to God Himself.

In God's fourth communication with Jacob, He said,

"Arise, go up to Beth-el, and dwell there: and make there an altar unto God, that appeared unto thee when thou fleddest from the face of Esau thy brother" (Gen. 35:1). Each previous communication that God had had with Jacob was for the purpose of establishing and restoring him. Jacob had a restless faith, and he needed to become established in his faith. In God's fourth communication with Jacob, He gave him the final call for complete separation. There was no other place Jacob could go. His only alternative was to flee to God. But to flee to God is to go forward with God.

God's call for Jacob to return to the land of his fathers was given on several occasions. After Jacob had spent 20 years with Laban, God told him, "Return unto the land of thy fathers, and to thy kindred; and I will be with thee" (31:3). When Jacob was returning and was on the border of the land, God appeared to him and said, "I am the God of Bethel, where thou anointedst the pillar, and where thou vowedst a vow unto me: now arise, get thee out from this land, and return unto the land of thy kindred" (v. 13). In Genesis 35:1 God once more, and with great emphasis, commanded Jacob to return to Bethel.

Jacob's experience at Shechem, when he had no place to turn but to God, was similar to the experience the nation of Israel had later. Under the leadership of Moses, the nation was fleeing Egypt, but they were hemmed in on all sides. The Red Sea was in front of them, the mountains were on one side, the desert was on the other, and the Egyptians were pursuing behind them. They had only one way to go, and that was to obey God and cast themselves completely on Him. As a result, He led them through the Red Sea without casualty.

Jacob Makes Haste

For Jacob, the patient chastening of a loving Heavenly Father had achieved its purpose: Jacob quickly did as God told him. God had met Jacob at Peniel, had changed his name and had made great promises to him. Some great advances were made in Jacob's life at Peniel, but a great time of crisis still followed. Jacob fell into deep sin after the mountaintop experience at Peniel. It was extremely difficult for him to learn the lessons of God, so God had to allow him and his family to fall into great reproach to cause them to see the need of returning to Bethel.

God's purpose had been accomplished—Jacob did not linger any longer. In God's command for Jacob to return to Bethel, He reminded him that it was the place where He had met him when he was fleeing from Esau. Once Jacob fully remembered Bethel, he also realized how far he had really fallen. In Shechem he had grown too accustomed to sin. His backslidden condition and the unregenerate people around him had clouded his vision so that he could not see the standards of God.

Today, many Christians are in the same condition. We attend our local churches regularly, but somehow we are blinded to the way we are going. The age of secularization has affected us to the extent that we cannot see the time we are wasting, which could be profitably spent for God.

Once Jacob had a renewed vision of the God of Bethel, it stirred him to quick action. The memory of past sins and what he had reaped from them drove him toward Bethel.

Perhaps this is how God is working in your life. Has He had to bring many difficulties and much suffering into your life to cause you to want to return to fellowship with Him? If you have not yet come to this place, how much more distress will God have to bring on you before you turn completely to Him? It is not always necessary that all of these hardships occur in your life. Jacob could have gone directly to Bethel from Peniel, but he spent 10 years in Shechem.

When God gave His call for complete separation—His command for Jacob to return to Bethel, Jacob lived up to his new name, Israel. "Then Jacob said unto his household, and to all that were with him, Put away the strange gods that are among you, and be clean, and change your garments: and let us arise, and go up to Beth-el; and I will make there an altar unto God, who answered me in the day of my distress, and was with me in the way which I went" (Gen. 35:2,3). Jacob's family obeyed: "They gave unto Jacob all the strange gods which were in their hand, and all their earrings which were in their ears; and Jacob hid them under the oak which was by Shechem" (v. 4). Jacob's family, including the sons who had committed murder, were suddenly obedient to him instead of rebellious. What made the difference? The difference was that Jacob was now speaking with the authority of God. God was in command and was speaking through Jacob to his family.

Strange Gods Put Away

In preparation for moving to Bethel, Jacob asked for three things. First, he asked that the strange gods be removed (Gen. 35:2). It would be impossible to worship idols and to worship at the altar of God at the same time. Jacob made it clear to his family that he intended to go to Bethel to build an altar to God (v. 3).

Because Jacob asked for the idols, or strange gods, they gave him their idols and also their earrings. It was the custom of the day to use earrings in pagan ceremonies. Aaron asked for the golden earrings when he made the golden calf (Ex. 32:2). In referring to adulterous Israel, God said, "I will visit upon her the days of Baalim, wherein she burned incense to them, and she decked herself with her earrings and her jewels, and she went after her lovers, and forgat me, saith the Lord" (Hos. 2:13).

Remember, Rachel had stolen the idols of her father, Laban. There is no record that Jacob had said anything about these gods previously, but now he said, "Put away the strange gods" (Gen. 35:2). While he was out of fellowship with God, Jacob was so weak spiritually that he did not have a clear-cut witness for God. Our testimony will also be weak before the world if we are not in fellowship with God.

After the idols had been given to Jacob, he "hid them under the oak which was by Shechem" (Gen. 35:4). Jacob knew he would never dare to return to Shechem; so he buried the idols there. The things of Satan are never to be used in the service of God. They must be entirely given up and destroyed. It is impossible to consecrate and sanctify them to God's service. Have you had a burial service for the unholy things in your life?

The Bible speaks strongly against those who worship false gods and idols. The word "idol" refers to that which is wholly seen. Whenever we are living for what is visible instead of that which is unseen, we are idol worshipers. Thus, we see how easy it is to make idols of our work, our

recreation, our family and so forth. If our lives are devoted to
God, who is not seen, then we will have the right relationship
to those things that are seen. The attitude of believers should
be "We look not at the things which are seen, but at the
things which are not seen: for the things which are seen are
temporal; but the things which are not seen are eternal"
(II Cor. 4:18).

Cleansing Commanded

Jacob not only demanded that his family remove the
strange gods, but he also commanded them, "Be clean"
(Gen. 35:2). This command was in preparation for meeting
God. Jacob realized they had to be cleansed if they were to
meet God and have real fellowship with Him. For Jacob this
did not have to do with the cleansing of salvation, for he had
met God 30 years earlier at Bethel, which was probably the
time of his salvation. But Jacob was going back to Bethel to
meet God, and it was important for him to be clean. He also
demanded this cleansing of his family.

The means of cleansing for present-day Christians is
stated in I John 1:9: "If we confess our sins, he is faithful and
just to forgive us our sins, and to cleanse us from all unrighteousness." These may be sins of omission as well as sins of
commission, but verse 7 of the same chapter assures us, "If
we walk in the light, as he is in the light, we have fellowship
one with another, and the blood of Jesus Christ his Son
cleanseth us from all sin."

Do you really desire fellowship with God? If you do, meditate on Psalm 139. This psalm shows how God can look into
our hearts. He sees everything; He knows everything. God
even knows the words you are going to speak before you
speak them. Because of this, the Psalmist David prayed,
"Search me, O God, and know my heart: try me, and know
my thoughts: and see if there be any wicked way in me, and
lead me in the way everlasting" (vv. 23,24). David was ask-
ing God to put him to the test—to try him. If anything in his
life was grievous or injurious to God in any way, David was
determined to confess it and be cleansed from it.

Psalm 56:13 has been a blessing to me many times. The
psalmist told God, "For thou hast delivered my soul from

death: wilt not thou deliver my feet from falling, that I may walk before God in the light of the living?" If you have received Jesus Christ as Saviour, you can say with the psalmist, "Thou hast delivered my soul from death." As you live the Christian life, you need to make the rest of this verse your prayer: "Wilt not thou deliver my feet from falling, that I may walk before God in the light of the living?"

'Change Your Garments'

In addition to commanding that his household remove their idols and be clean, Jacob also commanded, "Change your garments" (Gen. 35:2). This action has an important spiritual application. Jacob's household had to put aside garments of self-righteousness. New Testament believers are commanded, "Put off concerning the former conversation the old man, which is corrupt according to the deceitful lusts; and be renewed in the spirit of your mind; and that ye put on the new man, which after God is created in righteousness and true holiness. Wherefore putting away lying, speak every man truth with his neighbour: for we are members one of another" (Eph. 4:22-25).

We who know Christ as Saviour have died with Him to the old self, and we need to appropriate the benefits of His death for our lives. Christ not only died for our sins, but also we died with Him to sin. Therefore, the believer is to "put off" the things of the old nature, the flesh. This is done by an act of faith (see Rom. 6:6,11-13).

After Jacob's instructions had been followed, "they journeyed: and the terror of God was upon the cities that were round about them, and they did not pursue after the sons of Jacob. So Jacob came to Luz, which is in the land of Canaan, that is, Beth-el, he and all the people that were with him" (Gen. 35:5,6). Because God was in command, He took all evil intentions from the enemies of Jacob so that he and those with him were not harmed. God has sovereign control, and when we obey Him, we reap the blessings of that control. No hand can be raised against God's saints when they are in the center of His will. "When a man's ways please the Lord, he maketh even his enemies to be at peace with him" (Prov. 16:7).

Jacob Builds an Altar

God protected Jacob, and he arrived safely at his destination. Bethel at last! Then Jacob "built there an altar, and called the place El-beth-el: because there God appeared unto him, when he fled from the face of his brother" (Gen. 35:7). Jacob did what he had told his household he would do when they were preparing to go to Bethel: "Let us arise, and go up to Beth-el; and I will make there an altar unto God, who answered me in the day of my distress, and was with me in the way which I went" (v. 3). At that time, Jacob was saying to his family, "I am going back to where I found God, and there I am going to build an altar to the God who has protected me these 30 years and has now led me back." That is exactly what Jacob did.

Jacob called his new altar at Bethel "El-beth-el." He had built an altar at Shechem and called it "El-elohe-Israel." His name for the altar at Shechem meant "God, the God of Israel." Israel was Jacob's spiritual name. In this we see the importance of recognizing God as our personal God. But when Jacob built the new altar at Bethel, he called it "El-beth-el," which means "the God of Beth-el." The word "Beth-el" means "the house of God." So "El-Beth-el" is literally "the God of the house of God." Jacob saw the Heavenly Father as the God of the whole house of God. Jacob saw Him as his personal God, and he also realized that He was the God of every believer, for He is the ever-present God of the house of God.

This truth has its parallel in the New Testament. Ephesians 1:22,23 says, "And hath put all things under his feet, and gave him to be the head over all things to the church, which is his body, the fulness of him that filleth all in all." Every believer is baptized into the Body of Christ. First Corinthians 12:12,13 says, "For as the body is one, and hath many members, and all the members of that one body, being many, are one body: so also is Christ. For by one Spirit are we all baptized into one body, whether we be Jews or Gentiles, whether we be bond or free; and have been all made to drink into one Spirit."

There is just one Head—Jesus Christ—and every believer is a member of His Body. Ephesians 4:15,16 emphasizes this truth: "But speaking the truth in love, may grow up into him in all things, which is the head, even Christ: from whom the whole body fitly joined together and compacted by that which every joint supplieth, according to the effectual working in the measure of every part, maketh increase of the body unto the edifying of itself in love."

In Genesis 28:19, after Jacob had a vision of the ladder that reached to heaven, he called the place "Beth-el," the house of God. But after he returned to Bethel, he built an altar and called it "El-beth-el," the God of the house of God. The latter indicated a far higher view of God. The first name emphasized the place, or house, of God, whereas the latter emphasized God Himself. God had become more real to Jacob. His desire had become like the Apostle Paul's of the New Testament: "That I may know him" (Phil. 3:10).

When Jacob returned to Bethel, he found things as he had left them. There, 30 years earlier, Jacob had felt so small in the sight of God. Now he had been brought back to that place where he had earlier found real fellowship with God. During his years away from Bethel, Jacob thought he had attained so much by outscheming others. He had become too important in his own estimation to realize his need of God.

When a person first enters God's service, he feels exceedingly small. He realizes he is nothing in the sight of God. But after much success, it is tempting to feel self-sufficient. Samuel told King Saul, "When thou wast little in thine own sight, wast thou not made the head of the tribes of Israel, and the Lord anointed thee king over Israel?" (I Sam. 15:17). Many of God's servants have to be set aside by Him because they do not remain small in their own sight.

Every believer should meditate frequently on James 4:6-10: "But he giveth more grace. Wherefore he saith, God resisteth the proud, but giveth grace unto the humble. Submit yourselves therefore to God. Resist the devil, and he will flee from you. Draw nigh to God, and he will draw nigh to you. Cleanse your hands, ye sinners; and purify your hearts, ye double minded. Be afflicted, and mourn, and weep: let your laughter be turned to mourning, and your joy to heaviness. Humble yourselves in the sight of the Lord, and he shall lift you up."

When Jacob came back to Bethel, he was returning to the

joy of his salvation. His years away from God had brought
great agony of soul, even as David's sin brought great
anguish to him and caused him to pray, "Restore unto me the
joy of thy salvation" (Ps. 51:12).

God Appears to Jacob

After Jacob built the altar to God, "God appeared unto
Jacob again, when he came out of Padan-aram, and blessed
him" (Gen. 35:9). Jacob received a new revelation from God
when he returned to Bethel. Reconciliation had been completed. This was the fifth communication God had with
Jacob. In it, He ratified the covenant He had made with
Abraham and had later confirmed to Isaac. God told Jacob,
"Thy name is Jacob: thy name shall not be called any more
Jacob, but Israel shall be thy name: and he called his name
Israel. And God said unto him, I am God Almighty: be fruitful and multiply; a nation and a company of nations shall be
of thee, and kings shall come out of thy loins; and the land
which I gave Abraham and Isaac, to thee I will give it, and to
thy seed after thee will I give the land" (vv. 10-12).

The princeliness of Jacob was restored! God called him
Israel instead of Jacob. Ten years earlier God had changed
Jacob's name to Israel, but Jacob had not appropriated his
position. So also, when we received Jesus Christ as Saviour
we were called "saints" and "sons of God." But it is possible
that we have never appropriated the provisions God has
made for our lives. Positionally, Jacob had a new name, but
he had been living in a backslidden state. Then he came back
to Bethel.

From this time forward Jacob did not backslide to his old
life of scheming and deception. He applied faith and appropriated the provisions of God. As a result, in Hebrews 11 his
name is mentioned in the gallery of people of faith, along
with Abraham and Isaac (vv. 17-21).

When Jacob returned to Bethel, his communion and
prayer life were reestablished. Genesis 35:13 says, "And God
went up from him in the place where he talked with him."
After Jacob had made things right in his life, he was able to
commune freely with God.

Have you also experienced the spiritual dryness that
comes from a lack of communion with God? Are there things

in your life that need to be confessed to God? If so, apply
I John 1:9, and as you appropriate His forgiveness and
cleansing, you will again know the sweetness and blessing
that comes from talking and communing with God. How
wonderful it is to be on good speaking terms with our God!

A Divine Ebenezer

After God had gone up from the place where He and Jacob
had talked, "Jacob set up a pillar in the place where he talked
with him, even a pillar of stone: and he poured a drink-
offering thereon, and he poured oil thereon. And Jacob
called the name of the place where God spake with him,
Beth-el" (Gen. 35:14,15). Out of gratitude Jacob established a
memorial to God—a divine Ebenezer. God had recovered His
wayward child; Jacob was established spiritually. God knew
from the beginning that this would be the result. That is why
He was long-suffering and continued to work with Jacob.

The outworking of God's purpose for all of our lives is seen
in Romans 8:28,29: "And we know that all things work
together for good to them that love God, to them who are the
called according to his purpose. For whom he did foreknow,
he also did predestinate to be conformed to the image of his
Son, that he might be the firstborn among many brethren."

God predestinates in the sense that He sees something
through to its end. Certainly this was true concerning Jacob.
Nothing about Jacob's life was wasted as far as being used
to accomplish God's purpose. Even Jacob's failures were
used by God to accomplish His desired end. Each of Jacob's
failures had an important educational value. The supreme
lesson we can learn from Jacob is that no failure need be
final. There is always hope in God.

No past failure makes it impossible for you to have the
approval of God. Failures are to be confessed to God, and
then you are to step out in faith for Him. The Apostle Paul
said, "Forgetting those things which are behind, and reaching forth unto those things which are before, I press toward
the mark for the prize of the high calling of God in Christ
Jesus" (Phil. 3:13,14). When a person receives Jesus Christ
as his Saviour, God begins to work in him, and nothing
deters Him from performing and finishing that work.

The principle by which God works in our lives is faith.

That which is important about faith is not its quantity but its object. Faith in itself is valueless, but faith in God is invaluable. God always honors faith, regardless of how feeble and trembling it may be.

Faith in God marked the difference between Jacob and Esau. God never pursued Esau to accomplish a great work in his life because Esau despised the things of God. Faith in God was not evident in Esau's life. Even Lot, who was a child of God, did not desire the deep things of God; so God did not do a great work in his life either.

In long-suffering He pursued Jacob because deep in his heart was a longing for the things of God—even though he often tried to obtain them by carnal means.

God Is Just

Even though God is a God of patience and love, He is also a God of justice. In bringing Jacob back to Himself, God made no allowance for His servant's sin. In fact, Hebrews 12:5-11 indicates that God is more strict with His own children because He wants to bring out the best in them. Because God is holy and just, He cannot overlook sin.

Jacob had made a solemn vow when he was at Bethel earlier: "If God will be with me, and will keep me in this way that I go, and will give me bread to eat, and raiment to put on, so that I come again to my father's house in peace; then shall the Lord be my God: and this stone, which I have set for a pillar, shall be God's house: and of all that thou shalt give me I will surely give the tenth unto thee" (Gen. 28:20-22). God had completely fulfilled His part, but Jacob had not fulfilled much of his part. Jacob needed to "repent, and do the first works" as Christ instructed the Church of Ephesus (Rev. 2:5).

When Jacob returned to Bethel, it was his pleasure to make things right with God. Jacob set up "a pillar of stone" (Gen. 35:14), which no doubt reminded him of his vow and the pillar of stone he had built previously at Bethel. Then Jacob "poured a drink-offering thereon, and he poured oil thereon." All of this indicates that he had the pleasure of fellowship with God. Jacob was fully restored, and he began to appropriate the provisions of God and to live in accordance with his name, Israel.

God performed a great work in Jacob. What has God been able to do with you? The following poem emphasizes God's loving patience:

He came to my desk with a quivering lip—
   The lesson was done.
"Dear teacher, I want a new leaf," he said—
   "I have spoiled this one."
In place of the leaf so stained and blotted
   I gave him a new one all unspotted.
And into his sad eyes smiled—
   "Do better now, my child."

I went to the throne with a quivering soul—
   The old year was done.
"Dear Father, hast Thou a new leaf for me?
   I have spoiled this one."
He took the old leaf, stained and blotted,
   And gave me a new one all unspotted,
And into my sad heart smiled—
   "Do better now, My child."

—Author Unknown

Chapter 12

The School of Sorrow

Sorrow is one of God's means to make permanent in our lives the lessons of grace He has taught us. God had been dealing with Jacob for 30 years, and now Jacob was back at Bethel where God wanted him to be. God began to make permanent—to press deep into his heart—the lessons He had taught him during those 30 years.

From the day Jacob fulfilled his vow at Bethel to the day he learned Joseph was alive and the ruler in Egypt, Jacob was scarcely out of the furnace of affliction.

God makes no mistakes. He knows what He is doing. Sorrow is not necessarily punishment, but it strengthens us in Him by perfecting our faith and confidence in Him. Sorrow is often used for spiritual training. Through the process of chastening, God makes us into the kind of sons He wants us to be. Sorrow is intended to yield the peaceable fruit of righteousness: "Now no chastening for the present seemeth to be joyous, but grievous: nevertheless afterward it yieldeth the peaceable fruit of righteousness unto them which are exercised thereby" (Heb. 12:11). The peaceable fruit of righteousness only comes after the chastening.

Rebekah's Nurse Dies

Jacob felt the chastening hand of God even while he was at Bethel. After returning to Bethel, "Deborah Rebekah's nurse died, and she was buried beneath Beth-el under an oak: and the name of it was called Allon-bachuth" (Gen. 35:8). Deborah was probably the nurse who went with Rebekah when she left home to marry Isaac (24:59).

Deborah's death perhaps represented a separation for Jacob from his past life. A link had been broken. Back at

Bethel, Jacob was now ready for God to deal the death blow on *anything* that could link his life to the old ways and keep him from God.

This truth is also important for us today. Colossians 3:1-4 says, "If [since] ye then be risen with Christ, seek those things which are above, where Christ sitteth on the right hand of God. Set your affection on things above, not on things on the earth. For ye are dead [have died], and your life is hid with Christ in God. When Christ, who is our life, shall appear, then shall ye also appear with him in glory." Galatians 2:20 says, "I am [have been] crucified with Christ: nevertheless I live; yet not I, but Christ liveth in me: and the life which I now live in the flesh I live by the faith of the Son of God, who loved me, and gave himself for me."

Jacob's Wife Dies

Then Rachel, Jacob's beloved wife, died while they were enroute to Ephrath (Bethlehem). "Bethlehem" means "the place of food." Jacob was traveling from the house of God (Bethel) to the house of food (Bethlehem). Genesis 35:16 says, "And they journeyed from Beth-el; and there was but a little way to come to Ephrath: and Rachel travailed, and she had hard labour." Note that there was only "a little way" between Bethel and Bethlehem. Although these were literal cities, they point out a principle. The house of God and the house of bread, or food, are closely connected. When we put God first in everything, He provides for our needs. Christ Himself told His disciples, "Seek ye first the kingdom of God, and his righteousness; and all these things shall be added unto you" (Matt. 6:33).

When Rachel "was in hard labour, . . . the midwife said unto her, Fear not; thou shalt have this son also. And it came to pass, as her soul was in departing, (for she died) that she called his name Ben-oni: but his father called him Benjamin. And Rachel died, and was buried in the way to Ephrath, which is Beth-lehem" (Gen. 35:17-19).

Rachel named the child "Ben-oni" which means "son of my sorrow." However, Jacob named the child "Benjamin," which means "son of the right hand." Rachel's death was one of Jacob's deepest sorrows. She died sorrowing, but he triumphed in faith and called the child "son of the right hand."

Jacob took a victorious stand for God in spite of the fact that the most precious person in his life had been taken. Rachel's death and burial broke Jacob's main link with his past carnal life at Haran. He had gone there to get a wife and had been guilty of many carnal actions. "Jacob set a pillar upon her grave: that is the pillar of Rachel's grave unto this day" (v. 20). Jacob established a pillar in remembrance of the one who had been so very precious to him.

Because Jacob had returned to Bethel and had been fully restored to fellowship with God, he was now able to fulfill the second part of God's command: "Return . . . to thy kindred" (31:3). Thus, Jacob was on his way to his father, Isaac, who lived in Mamre. That is where Jacob was going when Rachel died in childbirth along the way.

Reuben's Sin

As Jacob and his family continued on their way to Mamre, his firstborn, Reuben, committed a great sin. The Bible says, "And Israel journeyed, and spread his tent beyond the tower of Edar. And it came to pass, when Israel dwelt in that land, that Reuben went and lay with Bilhah his father's concubine: and Israel heard it" (Gen. 35:21,22). Three times in these two verses Jacob is referred to by his new name, Israel. Jacob's life was now characterized by his new name.

When Reuben committed fornication with the concubine, "Israel heard it" (v. 22). Earlier when Jacob had learned of his sons' wickedness, he did nothing about it. But in Reuben's case, Israel was concerned about the things of God and did not let the sin go unpunished. Although it is not recorded in Genesis 35 how Jacob judged Reuben's sin, what he did was recorded later. Jacob said, "Reuben, thou art my firstborn, my might, and the beginning of my strength, the excellency of dignity, and the excellency of power: unstable as water, thou shalt not excel; because thou wentest up to thy father's bed; then defiledst thou it: he went up to my couch" (49:3,4). Reuben, as the firstborn, had rightful possession of the birthright, but Jacob said, "Thou shalt not excel." Jacob thoroughly judged Reuben's sin and took away his birthright.

Reuben's birthright was given to Joseph. This is evident from I Chronicles 5:1,2: "Now the sons of Reuben the first-born of Israel, (for he was the firstborn; but, forasmuch as he defiled his father's bed, his birthright was given unto the sons of Joseph the son of Israel: and the genealogy is not to be reckoned after the birthright. For Judah prevailed above his brethren, and of him came the chief ruler; but the birthright was Joseph's)."

Isaac Dies

Finally, Jacob arrived at his father's home in Mamre: "Jacob came unto Isaac his father unto Mamre, unto the city of Arbah, which is Hebron, where Abraham and Isaac sojourned" (Gen. 35:27). Jacob had not seen his father for at least 30 years. What a reunion they must have had! During the next 13 years Jacob cared for his father. Then we are told, "The days of Isaac were an hundred and fourscore years. And Isaac gave up the ghost, and died, and was gathered unto his people, being old and full of days: and his sons Esau and Jacob buried him" (vv. 28,29). The death of Isaac meant Jacob's separation from the past generation. The responsibility of the family was now entirely his. He had deceived Esau out of the birthright and had stolen the blessing many years earlier, but now the birthright was his by divine appointment—and so was the responsibility.

My father's funeral was a sobering experience for me. I was suddenly overwhelmed with the thought that the previous generation was gone. As the oldest in the family and the only son, I realized I had a special responsibility to carry on in behalf of the family. One of the last things my father said to me was "There is Mother, and there are your younger sisters." Thus I, too, inherited a special responsibility at the death of my father.

In the account of Isaac's death, it is precious to see that Esau and Jacob had apparently been reconciled: "His sons Esau and Jacob buried him" (v. 29). Death is often a great reconciler. Esau had said years earlier, "The days of mourning for my father are at hand; then will I slay my brother Jacob" (27:41). But Isaac did not die as soon as was expected, and by the time he did, Esau and Jacob were seemingly reconciled.

Concerning Esau, Genesis 36:6-8 says, "And Esau took his wives, and his sons, and his daughters, and all the persons of his house, and his cattle, and all his beasts, and all his substance, which he had got in the land of Canaan; and went into the country from the face of his brother Jacob. For their riches were more than that they might dwell together; and the land wherein they were strangers could not bear them because of their cattle. Thus dwelt Esau in mount Seir. Esau is Edom." Esau completely separated himself from the birthright heritage that now belonged to Jacob. Jacob (Israel) experienced total separation to God. Up until this time he was separated *from* the things of the world, but now he was separated *to* God.

Consider all that Jacob buried, as recorded in Genesis 35. First, he buried the idols that were given him by his household (v. 4). Second, he buried Deborah, Rachel's nurse. Third, he buried Rachel—his major link with his past carnal life. Fourth, he buried Isaac—the last link with the past generation. *Death* was written across this whole scene.

If we want to have true communion with God and serve Him in newness of power, we, too, must have the sentence of death written on our own desires and purposes. This is evident from Romans 6:11-14: "Likewise reckon ye also yourselves to be dead indeed unto sin, but alive unto God through Jesus Christ our Lord. Let not sin therefore reign in your mortal body, that ye should obey it in the lusts thereof. Neither yield ye your members as instruments of unrighteousness unto sin: but yield yourselves unto God, as those that are alive from the dead, and your members as instruments of righteousness unto God. For sin shall not have dominion over you: for ye are not under the law, but under grace." The sentence of death must be passed on the self-life if we are to be spiritual conquerors. This is an act of faith based on the accomplished work of Christ (Rom. 6:6).

Afflictions such as Jacob had are not to be viewed as judgments from God that result from divine anger. God does not act in such a way toward His own children. However, we are told, "Whom the Lord loveth he chasteneth, and scourgeth every son whom he receiveth" (Heb. 12:6). Even afflictions are among the love gifts of God, sent in faithfulness for our ultimate good. They are intended to wean our affections from the things of the earth so that we will cast ourselves completely on God to learn and experience His sufficiency. These afflictions are some of the "all things" of Romans 8:28. They yield "the peaceable fruit of righteousness unto them which are exercised thereby" (Heb. 12:11).

God usually deals with His children concerning the most tender aspects of their lives so there will be no rival to Him. Later, Jacob also experienced a severe trial concerning Joseph (Rachel's firstborn), who was taken from him and sold into Egypt.

When we humbly submit, God usually returns what He has taken from us or gives us something better. This principle was seen in the life of Abraham. God called on Abraham to offer Isaac, but God gave Isaac back to him. Jacob experienced this principle in his own life through the loss of loved ones. All of these experiences were used to mold Jacob into the man God intended him to be. Like John the Baptist, Jacob could have said, "He must increase, but I must decrease" (John 3:30). The following song emphasizes this so beautifully:

> Oh, the bitter pain and sorrow
>   That a time could ever be
> When I proudly said to Jesus—
>   "All of self and none of Thee."
>
> Yet He found me; I beheld Him
>   Bleeding on th' accursed tree;
> And my wistful heart said faintly
>   "Some of self and some of Thee."
>
> Day by day His tender mercy,
>   Healing, helping, full and free,
> Brought me lower, while I whispered—
>   "Less of self, and more of Thee!"
>
> Higher than the highest heavens,
>   Deeper than the deepest sea,
> "Lord, Thy love at last has conquered:
>   None of self and ALL of Thee!"
>   —Theodore Monod

A. J. Gordon said, "In every man's heart there is a throne and a cross. If Christ is on the throne, then self is on the cross. If self is on the throne, then Jesus is still on the cross."

Chapter 13

Victorious Faith in the Retiring Years

In his retiring years, Jacob might well have been described by the following words, "For which cause we faint not; but though our outward man perish, yet the inward man is renewed day by day. For our light affliction, which is but for a moment, worketh for us a far more exceeding and eternal weight of glory; while we look not at the things which are seen, but at the things which are not seen: for the things which are seen are temporal; but the things which are not seen are eternal" (II Cor. 4:16-18).

Jacob's retiring years evidenced the triumphs of God's grace in transforming a nearly impossible person. These latter years were the results of God's working in his life during his earlier life. God always showed Himself to be a God of mercy, long-suffering and grace.

In considering the grace of God, it is impossible to know which is the greater—the grace of God that gives the believer a perfect standing in Christ or the grace of God that bears with the believer in his failure to make his behavior correspond with his standing, or position, in Christ. As we consider both of these aspects, we will be overwhelmed with the realization that Christ died for our sins so that we could receive Him as Saviour, and that God has been so long-suffering, merciful and gracious to us throughout the years. How patiently God works with us until we produce the kind of fruit He desires.

Verses that especially emphasize the long-suffering and goodness of God toward us are Psalm 103:10-14: "He hath not dealt with us after our sins; nor rewarded us according to our iniquities. For as the heaven is high above the earth, so great is his mercy toward them that fear him. As far as the east is from the west, so far hath he removed our transgressions from us. Like as a father pitieth his children, so the Lord pitieth them that fear him. For he knoweth our frame; he remembereth that we are dust."

Joseph Is Sold

Concerning Jacob, the Word of God says that he "dwelt in the land wherein his father was a stranger, in the land of Canaan" (Gen. 37:1). Although Jacob was in the land of his fathers, he still experienced the heartaches of reaping what he had sown. His son Joseph was sold into Egypt, but Jacob was made to think differently by his sons.

Jacob's sons had "sold Joseph to the Ishmeelites for twenty pieces of silver" (v. 28). Then "they took Joseph's coat, and killed a kid of the goats, and dipped the coat in the blood; and they sent the coat of many colours, and they brought it to their father; and said, This have we found: know now whether it be thy son's coat or no. And he knew it, and said, It is my son's coat; an evil beast hath devoured him; Joseph is without doubt rent in pieces. And Jacob rent his clothes, and put sackcloth upon his loins, and mourned for his son many days. And all his sons and all his daughters rose up to comfort him; but he refused to be comforted; and he said, For I will go down into the grave unto my son mourning. Thus his father wept for him" (vv. 31-35). The apparent death of Joseph again struck one of Jacob's most tender spots, and victory was slow in coming.

Joseph had risen to a place of rulership in the land of Egypt and was responsible for conserving food for use during the famine. "Now when Jacob saw that there was corn in Egypt, Jacob said unto his sons, Why do ye look one upon another? And he said, Behold, I have heard that there is corn in Egypt; get you down thither, and buy for us from thence; that we may live, and not die" (42:1,2).

Jacob's action stood in great contrast to the action of his father, Isaac, and of his grandfather, Abraham. When these men had experienced famine, they left the place where they lived. Abraham went to Egypt, and Isaac went to the border of the land before God stopped him. But by this time Jacob had learned a great lesson. He was not going to leave the land where the house of God was—Bethel. Twice he sent his sons to Egypt to buy food, but he himself refused to leave the land. He had endured all the suffering he could possibly take, and he was not about to leave the land and invite more suffering.

When Simeon was retained in Egypt until the other brothers brought their youngest brother, Benjamin, to Egypt, it was almost more than Jacob could bear. Jacob told his sons, "Me have ye bereaved of my children: Joseph is not, and Simeon is not, and ye will take Benjamin away: all these things are against me" (v. 36). The eldest son, Reuben, told his father, "Slay my two sons, if I bring him not to thee: deliver him into my hand, and I will bring him to thee again" (v. 37). However, Jacob was insistent that Benjamin not go to Egypt. He said, "My son shall not go down with you; for his brother is dead, and he is left alone: if mischief befall him by the way in the which ye go, then shall ye bring down my gray hairs with sorrow to the grave" (v. 38).

Jacob Lets Benjamin Go

The situation became worse for Jacob and his family, and it became apparent they would have to go to Egypt if they were to get enough food to live. Jacob's son Judah suggested, "Send the lad [Benjamin] with me, and we will arise and go; that we may live, and not die, both we, and thou, and also our little ones. I will be surety for him; of my hand shalt thou require him: if I bring him not unto thee, and set him before thee, then let me bear the blame for ever" (Gen. 43:8,9).

Finally, Jacob agreed. The Bible says, "Their father Israel said unto them, If it must be so now, do this; take of the best fruits in the land in your vessels, and carry down the man a present, a little balm, and a little honey, spices, and myrrh, nuts, and almonds: and take double money in your hand; and the money that was brought again in the mouth of your sacks, carry it again in your hand; peradventure it was an oversight: take also your brother, and arise, go again unto the man: and God Almighty give you mercy before the man, that he may send away your other brother, and Benjamin. If I be bereaved of my children, I am bereaved" (vv. 11-14).

Jacob did not know that Joseph was the ruler in Egypt who had demanded to see his beloved brother Benjamin. When Jacob agreed to let Benjamin go, the Bible refers to Jacob as Israel (v. 11). The Spirit had won, and death to the self-life had finally conquered.

God never leaves believers unrewarded when they totally commit themselves to the Holy Spirit. The reaping is always beyond our highest expectations. This is emphasized in Romans 6:5,8: "For if we have been planted together in the likeness of his [Christ's] death, we shall be also in the likeness of his resurrection.... Now if we be dead with Christ, we believe that we shall also live with him."

We must die to self in order to really live. It is necessary to lose one's life in order to really find it. Jesus said, "Except a corn of wheat fall into the ground and die, it abideth alone: but if it die, it bringeth forth much fruit. He that loveth his life shall lose it, and he that hateth his life in this world shall keep it unto life eternal" (John 12:24,25). No matter how difficult circumstances may seem, nothing can separate us from the love of God, but rather "in all these things we are more than conquerors through him that loved us" (Rom. 8:37).

Joseph Is Alive!

Jacob discovered the reality of these principles also. Having been willing to give up everything, God returned not only what he had given up—Benjamin—but brought him the further blessing of knowing that Joseph was alive. Even more than that, Jacob and his family were invited to Egypt to feast under Joseph's supervision.

When Jacob's sons returned from Egypt and told him, "Joseph is yet alive, and he is governor over all the land of Egypt" (Gen. 45:26), the Word of God says that "Jacob's heart fainted, for he believed them not." Jacob's sons "told him all the words of Joseph, which he had said unto them: and when he saw the wagons which Joseph had sent to carry him, the spirit of Jacob their father revived: and Israel said, It is enough; Joseph my son is yet alive: I will go and see him before I die" (vv. 27,28). Notice that verse 27 refers to "Jacob": "the spirit of Jacob their father revived." However, verse 28 uses the name "Israel": "And Israel said."

Israel, not Jacob, put God first. His aching heart longed
for reunion with Joseph, but he did not go to Joseph until he
had done something extremely important. "Israel took his
journey with all that he had, and came to Beer-sheba, and
offered sacrifices unto the God of his father Isaac" (46:1).
Jacob did not go to Joseph without first communing with
God and seeking His permission. God met Jacob at this time,
and this was the seventh and final communication of God
with Jacob. "God spake unto Israel in the visions of the
night, and said, Jacob, Jacob. And he said, Here am I. And
he said, I am God, the God of thy father: fear not to go down
into Egypt; for I will there make of thee a great nation: I will
go down with thee into Egypt; and I will also surely bring
thee up again: and Joseph shall put his hand upon thine
eyes" (vv. 2-4). God gave Jacob a fourfold promise. First, God
said, "I will there make of thee a great nation" (v. 3). Second,
God promised, "I will go down with thee into Egypt" (v. 4).
Third, God assured Jacob, "I will also surely bring thee up
again" (v. 4). Fourth, God promised Jacob that "Joseph shall
put his hand upon thine eyes" (v. 4).

One of God's purposes in permitting Jacob and his family
to go to Egypt was so He could make a great people of them
there. In Canaan Jacob and his people might have intermar-
ried with the Canaanites and lost their distinction as God's
chosen people. Also, Jacob and his people might have been
destroyed by the Canaanites. In Egypt, however, they would
be a separate people, unmolested and allowed to multiply
greatly.

A Separate People

In Egypt, they would remain a distinct people through
whom God could work in fulfilling His promises. There was
no possibility that the Israelites would be absorbed by the
Egyptians because they were kept completely separate.
"Joseph said unto his brethren, and unto his father's house,
I will go up, and shew Pharaoh, and say unto him, My
brethren, and my father's house, which were in the land of
Canaan, are come unto me; and the men are shepherds, for
their trade hath been to feed cattle; and they have brought
their flocks, and their herds, and all that they have. And it
shall come to pass, when Pharaoh shall call you, and shall

say, What is your occupation? Then ye shall say, Thy servants' trade hath been about cattle from our youth even until now, both we, and also our fathers: that ye may dwell in the land of Goshen; for every shepherd is an abomination unto the Egyptians" (Gen. 46:31-34). This was part of God's plan to keep the Israelites separate from the Egyptians.

Pharaoh did as Joseph had hoped. He told Joseph, "The land of Egypt is before thee; in the best of the land make thy father and brethren to dwell: in the land of Goshen let them dwell: and if thou knowest any men of activity among them, then make them rulers over my cattle" (47:6). The Israelites needed a place to grow as a people and, at the same time, remain separate from the Egyptians. The attitude of the Egyptians toward shepherds was used of God to make both of these things possible.

Joseph introduced his aged father to Pharaoh: "Joseph brought in Jacob his father, and set him before Pharaoh: and Jacob blessed Pharaoh. And Pharaoh said unto Jacob, How old art thou? And Jacob said unto Pharaoh, The days of the years of my pilgrimage are an hundred and thirty years: few and evil have the days of the years of my life been, and have not attained unto the days of the years of the life of my fathers in the days of their pilgrimage. And Jacob blessed Pharaoh" (vv. 7-10).

Jacob was both bold and spiritually courageous before Pharaoh. Although Pharaoh probably considered Jacob an outcast because he was a shepherd, Jacob conducted himself as a child of God before Pharaoh. After all, Jacob was a son of the King of kings and an ambassador of the Most High. Jacob blessed Pharaoh—"the less [was] blessed of the better" (Heb. 7:7). Jacob realized his true position in God as he stood before Pharaoh.

Jacob also acknowledged his pilgrim status when he referred to the "years of my pilgrimage" (Gen. 47:9). Jacob viewed his entire life on earth as a pilgrimage. In this regard, he identified himself with Abraham and Isaac. Hebrews 11:9,10 says, "By faith he sojourned in the land of promise, as in a strange country, dwelling in tabernacles [tents] with Isaac and Jacob, the heirs with him of the same promise: for he looked for a city which hath foundations, whose builder and maker is God."

Jacob's Request

Genesis 47:27 says, "And Israel dwelt in the land of Egypt, in the country of Goshen; and they had possessions therein, and grew, and multiplied exceedingly." Just as God had promised, Jacob's people multiplied in Egypt. God was building a nation from Jacob. Jacob "lived in the land of Egypt seventeen years: so the whole age of Jacob was an hundred forty and seven years" (v. 28).

Jacob was old and about to die, but he did not want to be buried in Egypt. The Scriptures say, "The time drew nigh that Israel must die: and he called his son Joseph, and said unto him, If now I have found grace in thy sight, put, I pray thee, thy hand under my thigh, and deal kindly and truly with me; bury me not, I pray thee, in Egypt: but I will lie with my fathers, and thou shalt carry me out of Egypt, and bury me in their buryingplace. And he said, I will do as thou hast said. And he said, Swear unto me. And he sware unto him. And Israel bowed himself upon the bed's head" (vv. 19-31).

In faith and triumph Jacob looked forward to the time of the resurrection. His desire to be buried with his fathers was not mere sentimentality—it was the embracing of God's promise to possess the land. Jacob's besetting sin of unbelief had now been cast aside, and it was replaced with worship in faith. Jacob apparently wanted to be buried in the land so he could be resurrected from it. Jacob had an active faith.

Jacob Blesses Joseph's Sons

Before he died, "Israel said unto Joseph, Behold, I die: but God shall be with you, and bring you again unto the land of your fathers" (Gen. 48:21). Jacob was confident that all of his descendants would eventually be brought back into the land of his fathers. This act of worship in faith and the blessing of Joseph's two sons mark the climax of Jacob's faith. Hebrews 11:21 says, "By faith Jacob, when he was a dying, blessed both the sons of Joseph; and worshipped, leaning upon the top of his staff."

Before Jacob blessed Joseph's sons, he rehearsed for Joseph God's goodness in promise and fulfillment. Jacob told Joseph how God had said to him, "Behold, I will make thee fruitful, and multiply thee, and I will make of thee a multitude of people; and will give this land to thy seed after thee for an everlasting possession" (Gen. 48:4). Then Jacob claimed Joseph's sons as his own: "And now thy two sons, Ephraim and Manasseh, which were born unto thee in the land of Egypt before I came unto thee into Egypt, are mine; as Reuben and Simeon, they shall be mine" (v. 5). Having claimed them as his own sons, Jacob told Joseph, "Bring them, I pray thee, unto me, and I will bless them" (v. 9).

The account of Jacob's blessing Joseph's sons is recorded in Genesis 48:10-14: "Now the eyes of Israel were dim for age, so that he could not see. And he brought them near unto him; and he kissed them, and embraced them. And Israel said unto Joseph, I had not thought to see thy face: and, lo, God hath shewed me also thy seed. And Joseph brought them out from between his knees, and he bowed himself with his face to the earth. And Joseph took them both, Ephraim in his right hand toward Israel's left hand, and Manasseh in his left hand toward Israel's right hand, and brought them near unto him. And Israel stretched out his right hand, and laid it upon Ephraim's head, who was the younger, and his left hand upon Manasseh's head, guiding his hands wittingly; for Manasseh was the firstborn."

Joseph objected to what his father was doing: "When Joseph saw that his father laid his right hand upon the head of Ephraim, it displeased him: and he held up his father's hand, to remove it from Ephraim's head unto Manasseh's head" (v. 17). Because Manasseh was the firstborn and would customarily receive the major blessing, Joseph had brought his sons before Jacob in the position for Jacob to lay his right hand on Manasseh's head. But Jacob crossed his arms and did the opposite. Joseph said, "Not so, my father: for this is the firstborn; put thy right hand upon his head" (v. 18).

Jacob refused to do as Joseph suggested. He told Joseph, "I know it, my son, I know it: he also shall become a people, and he also shall be great: but truly his younger brother shall be greater than he, and his seed shall become a multitude of nations" (v. 19).

In this incident we see again God's sovereign choice of the younger son instead of the older one. Seth was chosen

instead of Cain, Shem instead of Japheth, Abraham instead
of Haran, Isaac instead of Ishmael, Jacob instead of Esau,
and now Ephraim instead of Manasseh.

In faith Jacob blessed Joseph's sons. His eyes were weak,
but because of faith his vision was strong.

Jacob Blesses His Sons

The end for Jacob had come. He called all of his sons
together for their final blessing. This was a fitting climax
that demonstrated the power of God's prevailing grace. One
by one Jacob blessed his children.

In all of his earlier life Jacob had been occupied with
himself; now he was occupied only with others. In his earlier
days he had been mainly concerned about planning for the
present; now he was occupied only with the future. "Jacob
called unto his sons, and said, Gather yourselves together,
that I may tell you that which shall befall you in the last
days" (Gen. 49:1). As Jacob was blessing his sons, he turned
his attention heavenward and said, "I have waited for thy
salvation, O Lord" (v. 18). One of the main things Jacob had
not been able to do during his lifetime was wait. But the
grace of God had completed a work in his life. What God had
begun, He finished. God had enabled Jacob to overcome the
sin that had beset him.

Jacob gathered his sons about him to bless them and to
foretell the future of their lives and of the tribes that would be
their descendants. Jacob said, "Gather yourselves together,
and hear, ye sons of Jacob; and hearken unto Israel your
father" (v. 2).

They were the "sons of Jacob" in that they were born
during his years of carnality when he was a schemer and a
supplanter. Even though they were the sons of Jacob, he
exhorted them to "hearken unto Israel your father." As
Israel, he was speaking the words of God. The predictions
given by Jacob in Genesis 49 are some of the most striking
ones found anywhere in the Old Testament. Jacob spoke in
love, but he was firm and truthful.

Reuben

Jacob's attention turned first to his oldest son, Reuben.
Jacob said, "Reuben, thou art my firstborn, my might, and

the beginning of my strength, the excellency of dignity, and the excellency of power: unstable as water, thou shalt not excel; because thou wentest up to thy father's bed; then defiledst thou it: he went up to my couch" (Gen.49:3,4). As the firstborn, the place of excellency and the position of dignity belonged to Reuben. However, his place of preeminence was forfeited because of the great sin he had committed earlier. That which was true of Reuben was also to be true of the tribe that would be born from him—"unstable as water, thou shalt not excel."

Because of Reuben's sin, the birthright was taken from him and given to Joseph, the firstborn of Rachel. The birthright involved a double portion of the inheritance and the scepter, which indicated the line of Christ. Whereas the double portion of the birthright went to Joseph, the scepter went to Judah.

This is also seen from I Chronicles 5:1,2: "Now the sons of Reuben the firstborn of Israel, (for he was the firstborn; but, forasmuch as he defiled his father's bed, his birthright was given unto the sons of Joseph the son of Israel: and the genealogy is not to be reckoned after the birthright. For Judah prevailed above his brethren, and of him came the chief ruler; but the birthright was Joseph's)." The double portion of Reuben's birthright was Joseph's (given to his sons, Ephraim and Manasseh), but the genealogy of Jesus Christ was to come through Judah.

Judah

In blessing Judah, Jacob said, "Judah, thou art he whom thy brethren shall praise: thy hand shall be in the neck of thine enemies; thy father's children shall bow down before thee. Judah is a lion's whelp: from the prey, my son, thou art gone up: he stooped down, he couched as a lion, and as an old lion; who shall rouse him up? The sceptre shall not depart from Judah, nor a lawgiver from between his feet, until Shiloh [Jesus Christ] come; and unto him shall the gathering of the people be" (Gen. 49:8-10).

Reuben did not excel, but Judah prevailed over his brothers. From Reuben's tribe came no judges, kings or prophets— those who excelled. However, many of the tribe of Judah excelled, and from this tribe was born the Lord Jesus Christ.

The double portion of the birthright that was given to Joseph was to remain his forever. In Ezekiel 47:13, which gives the borders of the land in the millennial age, God said, "This shall be the border, whereby ye shall inherit the land according to the twelve tribes of Israel: Joseph shall have two portions."

Simeon and Levi

When Jacob was delineating the characteristics of his sons and of those who would be their descendants, he said, "Simeon and Levi are brethren; instruments of cruelty are in their habitations. O my soul, come not thou into their secret; unto their assembly, mine honour, be not thou united: for in their anger they slew a man, and in their selfwill they digged down a wall. Cursed be their anger, for it was fierce; and their wrath, for it was cruel: I will divide them in Jacob, and scatter them in Israel" (Gen. 49:5-7).

These two sons had murdered the men at Shechem after the men had been circumcised. Jacob had told his sons at that time, "Ye have troubled me to make me to stink among the inhabitants of the land" (34:30). Now Jacob said that they would be scattered among their brothers: "I will divide them in Jacob, and scatter them in Israel" (49:7). This was exactly what happened. Simeon did not receive a special portion of the land for himself, but he had to dwell with his brothers. Neither did Levi receive a special portion, but he received cities where his tribe was to live. Although Levi had greatly sinned against the Lord, his descendants later took a stand for God that resulted in blessing for their tribe. The incident involved is recorded in Exodus 32. Moses had not returned from the mountaintop as quickly as the Israelites had expected, so they urged Aaron to make gods for them because they did not know what had happened to Moses. Aaron told the people, "Break off the golden earrings, which are in the ears of your wives, of your sons, and of your daughters, and bring them unto me" (v. 2). These were brought to Aaron and "he received them at their hand, and fashioned it with a graving [engraving] tool, after he had made it a molten [melted] calf: and they said, These be thy gods, O Israel, which brought thee up out of the land of Egypt" (v. 4).

When Moses returned from the mountaintop and saw what had taken place, he "stood in the gate of the camp, and said, Who is on the Lord's side? let him come unto me. And all the sons of Levi gathered themselves together unto him. And he said unto them, Thus saith the Lord God of Israel, Put every man his sword by his side, and go in and out from gate to gate throughout the camp, and slay every man his brother, and every man his companion, and every man his neighbour. And the children of Levi did according to the word of Moses" (vv. 26-28).

The sons of Levi did not participate in the sin of making the golden calf. Instead, they were on the Lord's side and did as Moses instructed. In the grace of God, the Levites were chosen for the priesthood and were given cities among all the people, but they were not given a separate inheritance of the land.

Jacob's Final Charge

Jacob gave a special blessing to each of his sons. Genesis 49:28 says, "All these are the twelve tribes of Israel: and this is it that their father spake unto them, and blessed them; every one according to his blessing he blessed them." None was overlooked. Jacob spoke faithfully about the temporal results of the sins of some of them, but each one was specially blessed.

Having blessed them, Jacob gave them a final charge: "I am to be gathered unto my people: bury me with my fathers in the cave that is in the field of Ephron the Hittite, in the cave that is in the field of Machpelah, which is before Mamre, in the land of Canaan, which Abraham bought with the field of Ephron the Hittite for a possession of a burying-place. There they buried Abraham and Sarah his wife; there they buried Isaac and Rebekah his wife; and there I buried Leah" (vv. 29-31). Jacob (Israel) realized that Egypt was not to be his final resting place. God had promised that Jacob would return to the land of his fathers. Therefore, Jacob gave instructions to his sons to carry him back to the land where he would wait for the resurrection. He, too, "looked for a city which hath foundations, whose builder and maker is God" (Heb. 11:10).

Jacob's Death and Burial

"When Jacob had made an end of commanding his sons, he gathered up his feet into the bed, and yielded up the ghost, and was gathered unto his people" (Gen. 49:33). This was the final scene for this man who had become great in the sight of God and in the sight of the world. Everything was now accomplished. The last counsel and the last blessing had been given. The last charge had been delivered to his sons. Then he "yielded up the ghost, and was gathered unto his people." Jacob's death was the death of a believer. He yielded his spirit to God and was reunited with his own people in the grave.

The funeral procession from Egypt to Canaan was undoubtedly one of the greatest funeral processions of all time. It covered a distance of 200 to 300 miles, depending on which road they took.

Observe the people involved in the funeral procession. Pharaoh gave permission to Joseph, saying, "Go up, and bury thy father, according as he made thee swear. And Joseph went up to bury his father: and with him went up all the servants of Pharaoh, the elders of his house, and all the elders of the land of Egypt, and all the house of Joseph, and his brethren, and his father's house: only their little ones, and their flocks, and their herds, they left in the land of Goshen. And there went up with him both chariots and horsemen: and it was a very great company" (50:6-9).

It is significant that even the servants of Pharaoh traveled from Egypt to Canaan in the funeral procession. Of this great company of people the Scriptures say, "They came to the threshing-floor of Atad, which is beyond Jordan, and there they mourned with a great and very sore lamentation: and he [Joseph] made a mourning for his father seven days" (v. 10).

What a striking sight this was to the Canaanites! "When the inhabitants of the land, the Canaanites, saw the mourning in the floor of Atad, they said, This is a grievous mourning to the Egyptians: wherefore the name of it was called Abel-mizraim, which is beyond Jordan" (v. 11). This was a climaxing testimony in death that crowned the final faith of God's man, Israel. God had won His man by love, mercy and grace. The Egyptians and the Canaanites were not without a witness of what God had done and could do.

Abraham, Isaac and Jacob had "looked for a city which hath foundations, whose builder and maker is God" (Heb. 11:10). These patriarchs were not satisfied with transitory promises. They were occupied with the thoughts of coming resurrection. Jesus Christ Himself said, "But as touching the resurrection of the dead, have ye not read that which was spoken unto you by God, saying, I am the God of Abraham, and the God of Isaac, and the God of Jacob? God is not the God of the dead, but of the living" (Matt. 22:31,32).

The Christian is inspired by the hope of the resurrection; the grave is not his goal. First Thessalonians 4:16-18 says, "For the Lord himself shall descend from heaven with a shout, with the voice of the archangel, and with the trump of God: and the dead in Christ shall rise first: then we which are alive and remain shall be caught up together with them in the clouds, to meet the Lord in the air: and so shall we ever be with the Lord. Wherefore comfort one another with these words."

In the Book of the Revelation, the Apostle John wrote: "And I John saw the holy city, new Jerusalem, coming down from God out of heaven, prepared as a bride adorned for her husband. And I heard a great voice out of heaven saying, Behold, the tabernacle of God is with men, and he will dwell with them, and they shall be his people, and God himself shall be with them, and be their God. And God shall wipe away all tears from their eyes; and there shall be no more death, neither sorrow, nor crying, neither shall there be any more pain: for the former things are passed away. And he that sat upon the throne said, Behold, I make all things new. And he said unto me, Write: for these words are true and faithful" (21:2-5).

An all-inclusive invitation is given in Revelation 22:17: "And the Spirit and the bride say, Come. And let him that heareth say, Come. And let him that is athirst come. And whosoever will, let him take the water of life freely." The Apostle John concluded the Book of the Revelation with the words: "He which testifieth these things saith, Surely I come quickly. Amen. Even so, come, Lord Jesus. The grace of our Lord Jesus Christ be with you all. Amen" (vv. 20,21).

If God should call you from this life today, would you be able to say with the Apostle Paul, "I have fought a good fight, I have finished my course, I have kept the faith: hence-forth there is laid up for me a crown of righteousness, which the Lord, the righteous judge, shall give me at that day: and not to me only, but unto all them also that love his appearing" (II Tim. 4:7,8)?

Jacob in Retrospect

Jacob is probably the most controversial character in the Bible. His weaknesses attract us because they cause him to appear more human. We feel he was more like we are. In Jacob, God's grace and patience resulted in a marvelous demonstration of what He can do with a person because He never wearies or gives up. If you are discouraged or broken-hearted over failure, never forget that God loves you and will not stop working to bring out His best in you. Remember, the God of Jacob is your God. He is unchanging, for He is "the same yesterday, and to day, and for ever" (Heb. 13:8).

Through the many tests and trials that God brought into Jacob's life, He brought forth a man who is in the gallery of the heroes of faith. He calls Himself "the God of Jacob," and He is our God also. Twice in one psalm the psalmist exclaimed, "The Lord of hosts is with us; the God of Jacob is our refuge. Selah" (Ps. 46:7,11).

Jacob's Diversified History

Jacob's life may be divided into nine stages during which he was trained and disciplined. First, Jacob's life at home was controlled by his strong-minded and self-willed mother, Rebekah. Her qualities were family characteristics, for Laban was the same way. Jacob also turned out to be a strong-minded, self-willed individual.

Second, Jacob reached a crisis at Bethel, where he met God for the first time in a personal way. This seems to have been the time of his conversion and of realizing that God was undertaking for his life—for him personally.

Third, Jacob received training and discipline while he was with his uncle Laban. God used Laban to show Jacob exactly what he himself was like. This stage of Jacob's life lasted 20 years.

Fourth, Jacob's long night at Peniel was a major turning point in his life, for there he began his life of surrender to God's commands. He did not always let God control his life after that time, but he made giant strides in his walk with the Lord because of his attitude of surrender.

Fifth, Jacob's mountaintop experience at Penial was followed by serious backsliding at Shechem. This backsliding resulted in great sorrow and trials for himself and his family. While living there, his daughter was raped and his sons committed murder in revenge.

Sixth, Jacob finally returned to Bethel and was restored to godly favor and fellowship. From this time on he constantly advanced in spiritual growth and maturity.

Seventh, there followed years of deep sorrow and suffering for Jacob, which strengthened and mellowed him.

Eighth, he was reunited with his son Joseph and enjoyed the restful and fruitful years in Egypt. All of Jacob's life he had had a restless faith, but in Egypt he developed a "resting" faith.

Ninth, Jacob's life was climaxed by his final great pronouncement of faith and triumph, by a peaceful death and by a great testimony even in his burial.

Of these nine periods of Jacob's life, three were especially crucial. His vision at Bethel was crucial in that it was no doubt the time of his regeneration. His struggle at Peniel was crucial because there he began his life of surrender to God's commands. His return to Bethel was crucial because he became established in true spiritual warfare for the Lord.

Jacob's Diversified Character

In Jacob's life there were two completely divergent qualities; yet there was a blending of them. He desired the things of God, but he used carnal means to obtain God's blessing.

In his youth, Jacob had the intense ambition to be the head of the family and to inherit the promises. In his old age, he had a remarkable quietness and gentleness of disposition.

Jacob seemed to have a deep understanding and full appreciation of God's covenant, but the sad aspect of his self-seeking disposition seemed to stop at nothing to gain its ends.

He had a deep love that centered in his mother, his wife

and his two sons, but he was also a cautious, suspicious individual who mistrusted everyone except himself.

Jacob had high aims and worked toward important goals, but he stooped to the most contemptible means of attaining his goals.

Jacob experienced slow progress in allowing the new nature (Israel) to control the old nature (Jacob). His old nature was never eradicated, but it was slowly subdued as his life took on more of the characteristics of Israel and fewer of the characteristics of Jacob. The transforming of Jacob into Israel was a slow process.

From the very first, Jacob's heart was set on the possessions included in the covenant of God that was given to his forefathers. He knew it was God's purpose that he should inherit the possessions. In the closing years of his life, the many years of severe discipline bore abundant fruit, and he emerged in strength and glory of character and life. At last he was more concerned about the Giver than about the gifts.

Jacob's Diversified Training

Jacob passed through *the school of sorrow and suffering*. He reaped what he had sown. His many serious mistakes took their toll on his life. He had deep sorrow because of the loss of his loved ones. He experienced many severe disappointments. He worked seven years for Rachel, but his father-in-law cheated him, and he had to work another seven years for her. Then there was Reuben's sin and Simeon's and Levi's treacheries. Jacob also experienced much heartache because of Joseph's being sold into slavery in Egypt and because of the demand that Benjamin be sent to Egypt with his other sons during the famine.

Jacob also experienced *the school of God's providence*. As God performed His work in him, Jacob became a man of quiet initiative, with abundant resources and a dauntless courage. Slowly but surely God directed Jacob into the path of spiritual usefulness. Jacob's resources were to be used by God and for God, but this was not true early in his life. Through God's constant and firm discipline, Jacob put all of his resources at God's disposal. At the end of his life, no one had more courage than Jacob. As Jacob stood before Pharaoh, not even Joseph could supersede him in courage.

Jacob also experienced *the school of divine grace*. This was the greatest and best training ground of Jacob's entire life. God's work in Jacob's life is possibly the outstanding example of His patience and long-suffering in dealing with His creatures. God's grace in Jacob's life stands out above all else and gives hope to the weakest, lowest and most hopeless believer. God is out to win, and win He will. "He which hath begun a good work in you will perform it until the day of Jesus Christ" (Phil. 1:6).

God's presence, full of grace and power, never left Jacob from the time of his vision at Bethel to the closing days of his life in Egypt. Jacob may not have always realized it, but God was constantly with him to perform His will through his life. God has said to us also, "I will never leave thee, nor forsake thee" (Heb. 13:5). Thus, we are able to understand why the person who has the God of Jacob for his refuge is blessed. What kind of a God do you have?

Concerning "the God of Jacob," W. H. Griffith Thomas wrote: "There is scarcely anything more striking in the whole of the Old Testament than the frequency of the title, 'the God of Jacob,' in the Psalms and in Isaiah. We could well understand God being the God of Israel, but to be called the God of Jacob is surely the crowning proof of Divine mercy and grace. What a remarkable point there is in the well-known words, 'The Lord of Hosts is with us; the God of Jacob is our refuge' (Ps. xlvi. 7). 'The Lord of Hosts' is the God of Providence, protecting against foes, overcoming difficulties, and providing for all emergencies, but 'the God of Jacob is our refuge' is very much more than this. It tells of His mercy and grace. The God of Jacob is a God of unwearying love, of unerring wisdom, of unfailing grace. He is our Refuge in spite of our sins, in the face of our failures, in view of our fears. And because He is all this He asks for our unreserved surrender, our unquestioning faith, our unflinching loyalty, our unfailing hope, and whispers in our hearts, 'Fear not thou worm Jacob ... I will help thee, saith the Lord, and thy Redeemer is the Holy One of Israel.' It is because God is the God of Jacob that we have such unbounded confidence in His mercy and grace, in His love and longsuffering. It tells us what grace can do for even the very worst of us. As a man said to a clergyman not long ago, 'I am cheered when I read the life of Jacob; for if the grace of Almighty God was able to straighten up that man, there must be some hope for me' " *(Genesis, A Devotional Commentary,* pp. 494, 495).

How wonderful to know that the God of Jacob is our God also! Claim Him as your own by faith. Rejoice in His love, mercy and grace. Triumph through His almighty power, for He works in you and through you by His indwelling presence. "Christ in you, the hope of glory" (Col. 1:27).